The Science Of Sticky Coaching
Ordinary Athletes Into Extraordinary

THE SCIENCE OF STICKY COACHING: HOW TO TURN ORDINARY ATHLETES INTO EXTRAORDINARY

How To Turn Ordinary Athletes Into Extraordinary

Joey Myers

Copyright © 2017 by Joey Myers

All rights reserved

For information about permission to reproduce selections from this book, write to joey@hittingperformancelab.com

Library of Congress Cataloging-in-Publication Data is available.

ISBN 1542860032

ISBN 978-1542860031

CATAPULT LOADING SYSTEM, SCIENCE OF STICKY COACHING, and HITTING PERFORMANCE LAB are trademarks or registered trademarks, all under license. All rights reserved.

Cover and back jacket design by Rann Dasko

PLEASE REVIEW ON AMAZON

Thank you for downloading my book, please review on Amazon so we can make future versions even better.

CONTENTS

Acknowledgements	ix
Introduction	1
1. Section 1, Chapter 1	13
2. Section 1, Chapter 2	16
3. Section 1, Chapter 3	18
4. Section 1, Chapter 4	21
5. Section 1, Chapter 5	23
6. Section 1, Chapter 6	28
7. Section 1, Chapter 7	31
8. Section 1, Chapter 8	34
9. Section 1, Chapter 9	36
10. Section 1, Chapter 10	38
11. Section 1, Chapter 11	41
12. Section 1, Chapter 12	45
13. Section 1, Chapter 13	47
14. Section 1, Chapter 14	51
15. Section 1, Chapter 15	54
16. Section 1, Chapter 16	56
17. Section 2, Chapter 1	60
18. Section 2, Chapter 2	61
19. Section 2, Chapter 3	65
20. Section 2, Chapter 4	68
21. Section 2, Chapter 5	77
22. Section 2, Chapter 6	80
23. Section 3, Chapter 1	84
24. Section 3, Chapter 2	87
25. Section 3, Chapter 3	91
26. Section 3, Chapter 4	94
27. Section 3, Chapter 5	97
28. Section 3, Chapter 6	102
29. Section 3, Chapter 7	106
30. Section 3, Chapter 8	108
Afterword	113
How To Teach 100-Pound Hitters To Consistently Drive The Ball 300-Feet Book	115
Books and References	117
Book Cliff Notes	118
About The Author	124

ACKNOWLEDGEMENTS

First and foremost I have to **thank my most loving and supportive wife and family**. I spent many of nights on a deadline, to get this book done, alone in our bedroom hacking away at the keyboard.

Tiffany Myers, who **I'm lucky to have snagged before some other hairy-backed-knuckle-dragger**, and with over 9 years of marriage, you complete me.

This is also for my 4 year old son Noah, and 9 month old daughter Gracen. You guys will learn the value of hard work on whatever passionate curiosity you find yourself in. Mommy and Daddy will help keep providing oxygen to that fire making it as big as you want it.

I want to thank Rann Dasco for the beautiful front and back cover design. You did a fantastic job girlie! **You made me feel like I had BIG shoes to fill with the content** ?

I also wanted to thank the coaches who helped me edit this "thing" back in 2013. Your advice and course corrections helped make this book what it is.

INTRODUCTION

Discover How-To Teach, What to Teach, and How Athletes Optimally Learn By Doing What the Top 1% of Coaches Do

My competitive edge from other coaches and instructors is that for the last decade I've done (and continue to do) a ton of scientific research and study on how humans effectively develop, move, and think.

Some coaches boast they have 30+ years of coaching experience, but what they really have is **the same one year of coaching experience repeated over thirty years**.

Besides being a part of the International Youth Conditioning Association, American Baseball Coaches Association, and a huge supporter of the Positive Coaching Alliance, I've spent almost eleven-plus years in the corrective fitness field. I have certifications from the National Academy of Sports Medicine (NASM), Corrective Exercise Specialist (CES), Functional Muscle Screen (FMS), and Yoga.

I'm a student of bio-mechanical geniuses like Paul Chek of the C.H.E.K. Institute, Charles Poliquin of Poliquin Performance, Drs. Gray Cook and Lee Burton are both Physical Therapists and are founders of the Functional Muscle Screen (FMS), Dr. W. Eric Cobb a Chiropractor and founder of Z-Health Performance, fascial body worker Thomas Myers and his book Anatomy Trains, Dr. Erik Dalton (another body worker) and his collaborative book Dynamic Body, Dr. Kelly Starrett a Physical Therapists founder and author of MobilityWOD.com and his book Becoming a Supple Leopard, and not to mention many other experts I will be referencing in the following pages.

Quick Notes on References

I'll be referencing different scholarly books and people on the subject of coaching, parenting, and teaching. In order to quickly get to the meat and potatoes of the book, I included a full explanation of sources and links to Amazon *(in case you want to purchase them)* at the end. Go to the Table of Contents and CLICK *"Books and References"*.

Why Great Parents Make Great Coaches...

In doing research for this book, I ran into a dilemma...I don't – at the time of this writing – coach baseball or softball teams. I mostly teach hitting through private instruction both online and off, I've coached a few soccer teams before my wife and I had kids, and have quite a bit of experience coaching groups in the fitness industry.

But then I thought about it...whether you're a team's coach, do private instruction, or are a teacher, it doesn't matter. **The principles of successful learning remain unchanged**.

Through my research, another synonym I threw in the melting pot was "parent." Parents are coaches as well as teachers. As a fairly new parent of one 4-year-old boy and 9-month-old baby girl, I can now see the connection.

What you'll find echoed throughout this book: **great coaching is actually a wolf in sheep's clothing for great parenting.** There's *doing things right*, and *doing the right things*. I'm going to *teach* you, thanks to the Top 1% of coaches, how-to effectively and efficiently coach young athletes.

How Does this Book Work?

I've split up *The Science Of Sticky Coaching* book into three parts:

- **KNOWLEDGE** (How-To Teach, Doing Things Right, "Effectiveness"): equipping inexperienced coaches, parents, and organizational leaders how to effectively run their associations and teams,
- **LEARNING** (How they learn) – optimizing how young athletes acquire new skills, and maintaining a rich soil for learning, AND
- **DEVELOPMENT** (What to teach, Doing the Right Things, "Efficiency"): how-to practice like you play, so you play like you practice.

Each book-part is split up into a simple metaphor I often use from the Heath brothers' book *Switch*, in which they refer to three aspects to change:

- **Guiding the Rider** (the planning brain),
- **Motivating the Elephant** (emotional ignition), and
- **Shaping the Path** (direction on where to go).

Before getting your elbows dirty, there is a vital issue we need to address with coaching young athletes…

DON'T DO this for Effective Coaching

"Winning!!" – Charlie Sheen

"If there's anything you could point out where I was a little different, it was the fact that I never mentioned winning." – John Wooden (UCLA Bruins 10-time national championship basketball coach in a 12-year span)

I had a heated run in with a parent (actually grand-parent) associated with my eight-year-old nephew's Little League All-Star Team back in 2013. At the game, my brother-in-law informed me how my nephew's team crushed another team 18-2 the night before. Come to find out, I knew the poor team's coaches pretty well (one was my Little League Coach back in the day).

Apparently, my nephew's coach **kept taking advantage of the other team's** inability to play catch, instructing his troops to take the extra base every chance they got – regardless of the score. Every base on ball was a chance to sprint to second base and watch the circus folly all over again.

My stomach knotted upon hearing this.

Before the start of the game, I was openly talking about my minor distaste for my nephew's coach running-up-the-score, when I noticed there was an older gentleman – on our side – whose **clearly disagreeing rabbit ears perked up**.

This opinionated old-timer went on to make the following arguments, much to my convincing otherwise:

- *"It's ALL about winning at 8 years old."*

- "Kids NEED to learn how to lose."
- "But the tournament rules say the team scoring the most runs gets to the championship game."
- "The coach on the other team would've done the same thing."

My rebuttals of the following fell on deaf ears:

- "It's not about winning at this age, it's about development."
- Questioning whether, "Kids need to learn how to lose, like, 18-2, really??"
- "What if the tournament rules said that if a hitter goes up and **punches the pitcher in the face**, you get ten extra runs, would you allow that?"…and
- "I know the character of the coach on the other team, and he would NOT have done that."…

An Ah-Ha Moment for Me

Upon reflection and after a two-day cool-off period when I didn't feel like punching my fist through a brick wall, I wrote down a few alarming trends I saw that day, and hear about constantly from my parents with young men and women at the 12 and under levels:

- We're more concerned with *winning* (what we CAN'T control), rather than *skill execution* and *development* (what we CAN control).
- We'd rather say "Good job!" to a young athlete (focus on foggy generalized outcomes) rather than you must've really worked hard to _____ (fill in the blank) – praise-for-effort language.
- And worst of all, **we'd rather protect our coaches' and parents' reputation** other than develop our athletes' character.

We may be familiar with numbers one and three above, but let me clarify number two. Whenever something doesn't make sense, I've learned to look at what the Science says…

So, **what's the problem with saying your kid is so** _____ (fill in the blank: "smart", "strong", or "awesome") – basically generalized unclear outcomes…

Remember when I said parenting, coaching, and teaching run along the same line? From the national bestselling book *Brain Rules for Baby*, by John Medina:

> "First, your child begins to perceive mistakes as failures. Because you told her that success was due to some static ability over which she had no control, she starts to think of failure (such as a bad grade) as a static thing, too — now perceived as a lack of ability. Successes are thought of as gifts rather than the governable product of effort.
> Second, perhaps as a reaction to the first, **she becomes more concerned with looking smart** than with actually learning something.
> Third, she becomes less willing to confront the reasons behind any deficiencies, less willing to make an effort. Such kids have a difficult time admitting errors. There is simply too much at stake for the future."

See what the problem is with focusing on "Winning?!" We CANNOT control it.

Your Kids WILL Fail

As you may know by now, the sport of baseball and softball are built on failure and making mistakes. Hitting a moving ball (not knowing pitch type, speed, and location beforehand) with repeatable power is THE hardest thing to do athletically. Period. End of discussion.

If kids are constantly told that they're winners…and how good they are…how smart they are…we as coaches and parents set them up to fall…HARD. And **without learning the proper perspective and necessary coping mechanisms**, they'll be sluggish to get back up.

I did get my verbal licks in with the opinionated man. Although, on later reflection – for me – it wasn't about winning the argument, but to clearly see the gaping wound on the face of every Little Leaguer and 12u Fastpitch Softball athlete playing in America today.

Let me be clear…

The gentleman at the game doesn't upset me, now. He was only a messenger. He **brought to my reality this broken coaching pattern**. Believe me, I'd thank him now, and possibly give him a kiss on the lips (like Bugs Bunny). Weird, yes, but I don't care.

12u athletes don't give a flying fart about winning. What they care about is:

- Having fun,
- Sugary snacks and drinks,
- Pizza after the game, and above all
- Pleasing adults.

It's the *parents* and *coaches* that condition them otherwise.

As Mike Matheny (manager of the St. Louis Cardinals) says in his Letter to Parents,

"It's ALL about the boys."

The Objective of This Course

LittleLeague.org's participation statistics following the 2008 season, reported 2.6 million Little Leaguers worldwide. A year prior, they reported 2.2 million worldwide. That's a **400,000 young athlete jump in one year**! Now in 2017, I've heard that number is up over 16-million for both baseball and softball participation worldwide!!

Although Little League participation stats show we're growing, it doesn't account for player retention within the sport. The reality is, we're losing athletes to other sports.

With this book, it is now my duty **to overhaul the way** Little League and 12u softball coaching is done, and to help organizations become more effective and efficient in running their leagues.

A blessing and a curse?

Anybody can coach baseball or softball – that's a good thing – so we have enough coaches to match the demand. It's also a problem because of what I call "low-entry coaching". Unlike soccer, and to my knowledge (I could be wrong), but most Little League and fast-pitch softball organizations **have little-to-NO certification training** that must be earned and paid for before having the responsibility of coaching a team.

Little to NO prior knowledge needed! Isn't that scary?

Also, a lot of this book will dive into how a coach's thinking and word usage make a heck-of-a-difference on how players perform.

As an example, one of my readers Andy Rando wanted me to make a mention of the difference in the 2012 Boston Red Sox versus 2013 because of a simple change in head coaching.

Terry Francona (Cleveland Indians head coach) led the Red Sox from 2004 to 2011 to winning two World Series titles during this span (2004 & 2007). According to Baseball-Almanac.com, **there were only two out of eight seasons**, in Francona's coaching span, where Boston didn't win ninety or more games (86-wins in 2006 & 89-wins in 2010).

Enter Bobby Valentine, a guy notorious for a big ego. The Red Sox finished 69-93 overall. I was tired of seeing guys like Big Papi and Dustin Pedroia getting thrown under the bus (or throwing Valentine under) on Sportscenter because of his coaching "style." Pedroia and Ortiz are both stand-up guys, so I knew something was up.

Then came John Farrell in 2013. Another Boston Red Sox world championship. They finished the regular season at 97-65.

Is it a coincidence once Valentine was dropped as head coach that the Red Sox made a third run for a World Series title in ten years?

You can draw your own conclusions. But what I do know at the Little League and 12u Fast-pitch levels, is that players are looking for coaches to be role models to them. Think great "parents". I think coaches at this level have a more difficult job than coaches at the MLB level. The glaring issue is most ARE NOT getting paid to put up with the junk that they do. The following pages will help to alleviate all the extra-curricular that goes on behind the scenes.

This book will be a step in the right direction. Here are some other challenges coaches WILL run into…

Critical Time in Athlete's Neuromuscular Development

In youth baseball and softball, there's been no systematic approach to movement development, which leads to a high risk for injury. This is leading to a record number of hip and knee injuries in female athletes once they get to High School.

WHY?

Well, according to David Epstein's book *The Sports Gene: Inside the Science of Extraordinary Athletic Performance*, it's because of how females are built…**wider hips make speed and agility less efficient on the body**.

And for boys, shoulder and elbow surgeries before they get to college! Baseball and softball are some of the most imbalanced sports an athlete can play!

There's a natural balance to human movement progression, and we'll talk about solutions in the coming pages of this book.

Under-Prepared Coaches

Have you ever seen this famous quote…?

> *"If you fail to prepare, then you prepare to fail."*

This leads to belittling, yelling, increased pressure to win, teaching through fear, no empathy, no patience, and negative criticism coaching.

As the dominoes fall, this leads to athletes experiencing:

- That they're never quite good enough,
- Low self-esteem – feeling lost and having no control,
- A low capacity for learning with a "threatening" coach – **we learn to survive, not survive to learn**, and
- Eventually early burnout – OR they may take on an alternative sport hoping the grass is greener on the other side.

Remember when I mentioned great parents make great coaches?

Studies show the divorce rate for new parents is above the national average of 60%...UNLESS, the pregnancy was planned, the couple had been together for quite some time, and the new parents had a loving support group. Imagine that, **prepared parents tend to stay together, and have happier homes**.

Prepared coaches can have the same affect on their teams, and we'll go over that in the coming Chapters.

Is Playing ONLY Baseball or Softball Okay?

This is from an IYCA email I received addressing the issue of specializing in one sport early on...

> *"Recently several researchers (Moesch, Elbe, Haube and Wikman) published a very interesting article in the Scandinavian Journal of Medicine and Sport Science examining just this theory and has amazing implications for the coaching in your program.*
>
> *The researchers asked elite athletes and near elite athletes to answer questions about their experiences in athletics regarding their training and practice throughout their career.*
>
> - *The near-elite athletes **actually accumulated more hours of training** than the elite athletes prior to age 15.*
> - *By age 18 the elite athletes had **accumulated an equal number of hours training** to the near elite athletes.*
> - *From age 18-21 elite athletes **accumulate more training hours** than near elite athletes.*
> - *Elite athletes said that they passed significant points in their career (first competition, starting a sport) at later dates than the near elite athletes.*
>
> *This reporting suggests that athletes do need to accumulate great amounts of hours training to get to an elite status, but also suggest that the critical time may not be extremely early in their career. Rather, it suggests that after a period of great diversification in athletic endeavors, athletes will ultimately be more successful."*

We're crafting elite athletes, NOT baseball or softball players. You'll be learning about what this means in this book.

"1 in 3 Children Considered Over-Weight or Obese"

Thanks in-part to the following:

- LOTS of daily sitting (school and home)
- Concerns over adolescent safety has eliminated "free neighborhood play"
- Video game addiction and technology boom
- **Incomplete physical education**
- Food void of nutrients
- Lack of manual labor
- Over-structured lives (too much going on!)
- Poor or lack of sports and training regimens, and
- Lack of sleep (recent studies point to this even more than kids being more sedentary).

You're going to learn how to do your part in the following pages.

Over-Coaching

In the book *The Talent Code*, author Daniel Coyle mentions that our goal as a coach/teacher/parent is to **progressively make ourselves unnecessary**. This means the less feedback we give, the better. There's a happy medium between too much and nothing at all.

I call it the Goldilocks Golden Rule…not too hot…not too cold…we want it just right.

You're going to learn how in this book.

Hyper-Parenting

According to John Medina's book *Brain Rules for Baby*, research from David Elkind, professor emeritus of child development at Tufts University, says there are **four types of over-achieving parents**:

1. Gourmet,
2. College-degree,
3. Outward-bound, and
4. Prodigy.

We'll address these later in the book. And I'll also be giving you an up-front agreement PDF you can share with your parents. Studies overwhelmingly show **smothering parents lead to poor performance**.

"NO Beginning Athlete Left Behind"

I ran a survey to my thousands of online subscribers, and found there's a huge gap between how high-level travel players and beginning players are treated.

Apparently, very few parents and coaches want to develop beginners because it requires "too much work" and "patience"…as one parent said to my friend Justin, who's a volunteer coach for a 12U travel baseball team in Bakersfield,

> "Why don't you just recruit developed players, so we can go to more tournaments, and win faster?"

Sound familiar?

I laughed. You'll learn **how-to inter-weave a development-focused team culture** in this book, which will help to educate parents. OR, act like a force-field keeping out parents who want to cut corners in developing their young athletes.

Is Talent Born OR Made?

I highly recommend David Epstein's book *The Sports Gene* mentioned earlier because the conclusion he came to in all his research is **that talent is BOTH nature AND nurture**. If you think it's one over the other, then you're DEAD WRONG.

Talent can be genetic, yes. But if you're *doing things right*, and *doing them the right way*, then you **won't have any trouble competing with the best in the world**.

Look at elite hitters like:

- Hank Aaron (6'0", 180lbs),

- Saduharu Oh (5"10", 175lbs, career home-run leader in Japan with 868 homers),
- Jose Bautista (6'0", 190lbs),
- Robinson Cano (6'0", 205lbs),
- Dustin Pedroia (5'8", 165lbs), and
- Andrew McCutchen (5'10", 185lbs)…

These are small guys that hit like big ones, and they definitely didn't win the genetic lottery. In other words, **you can teach high level mechanics, the right team fundamentals**, and still get results with smaller less developed kids with this book and my others. Take it from me, I've developed a reputation for helping hitters weighing around 100-lbs consistently drive the ball 300-feet.

And it's not just me, but I've also helped hundreds of coaches across the nation get the same – if not better – results than I'm getting. More on my hitting formula in the book *The Catapult Loading System* that's currently being sold on Amazon.

"Career Specialists Can't Externalize What They've Internalized" –Tim Ferriss

The internet is saturated with big name coaches and instructors boasting how they can get you to achieve "X" because they coached at the highest level for thirty years. When in reality, what these coaches really have, is the same one year of coaching experience repeated for 30 years.

We've seen guys like Tony Gwynn, the Ripken brothers, and Nomar Garciaparra give really generic advice on how to do what they did. Their advice is so vague, leaving too much up to the imagination, that the advice falls on deaf ears.

We've seen time and time again that there's a big difference in what a Major Leaguer *feels* that he's doing, and what we're seeing as *real* on slow motion video analysis. It's the *real* versus *feel* dilemma.

Like Mr. Tim Ferriss adds in his NY Times #1 Best Selling Book, the Four Hour Chef…

> *"The top 1% often succeed **despite how they train**, not because of it. Superior genetics, or a luxurious full-time schedule, make up for a lot."*

Not all of us can be in the top 1%. But in six-twelve months, we can certainly be a part of the top 5% in the world. So, who do we trust?

Those who look at the empirical research revealed through the scientific process…we'll be looking to just those studies and books in the following Chapters.

Material Beats Method (falling for the 10,000-hour to mastery rule)

In the YouTube age, there are flimsy regurgitated methods everywhere. Do this or that drill. Hit like this not like that. Throw like this, not like that. All this information has been passed down from generation to generation with zero proven science to back it. It can be very convincing.

And who's right?

The most sophisticated video? The **video with the most views**? The most popular talked about video?

Not necessarily. Great marketing can over-shadow terrible information. Just type "how to hit a homerun" into the YouTube search bar, and **watch the video** just under Domingo Ayala's. It's terrible! While you're at it, check out some of the comments below the video…people feel 'tricked' by smart marketing. But hey it's popular, receiving over 1.7 million views!

Have you heard this quote before by Ralph Waldo Emerson…?

*"As to the methods there may be a million and then some, but principles are few. **The man who grasps principles can successfully** select his own methods. The man who tries methods, ignoring principles, is sure to have trouble."*

Who do you listen to? Those who stand on the shoulders of giants. Those who look to proven Science. And we seek to do that in this book.

Raising Immoral Athletes

These days, youth athletes don't respect authority. They don't respect their coaches, teammates, competitors, umpires, and yes even parents (both theirs and others). Can I get an AMEN on that?!

According to John Medina in his book *Brain Rules For Babies*, all kids crave discipline and organization, even though they may not like to comply. They still **yearn for structure** (i.e. discipline and order).

Granted, not all coaches are effective. However, I still give the benefit of the doubt, because I think most coaches at the youth level just don't have the knowledge to develop and teach young athletes progressively. If these are taken care of, and we still have a bad apple? Then run for the hills.

In this book, you'll **learn three simple commandments** of raising a moral athlete.

Nice, Easy, & Pleasant Environment Shuts Off Motivation

This seems counter-intuitive, but the research says when we let young athletes play on the nicest most manicured fields, wear brand spanking new uniforms every season, and swing the most technologically advanced bats, then their **motivation to reach for the next level dramatically drops**.

I read an online quote the other day that came from Joe DiMaggio:

> *"A ball player has to be kept hungry to become a big leaguer. That's why no boy from a rich family **has ever made the big leagues**."*

Now, DiMaggio's comment may not be the correlation that leads to causation, because there are boys "from a rich family" that do make the Big Leagues.

However motivation and inspiration are two different things.

Like life change coach Tony Robbins says, *"Motivation is like a warm bath"*…it cools quickly. **Motivation is *pushing* someone in a direction, while inspiration *pulls* that person along their chosen path**. The latter being more powerful.

This may be why young athletes in developing countries like Curacao, Dominican Republic, Puerto Rico, and Cuba just "want it more." They're hungry to get off the island.

In this book, you'll discover a few tricks to keep your players inspired to succeed and progress to the next level, and how we may be hurting the development of our athletes. One simple idea will fix this!

The Power of Discipline, Organization, & Consequences

Legendary college baseball Coach Bob Bennett said one of the most influential coaches of his youth, was one who didn't know one lick about the game of baseball. However, what this coach did know was how to teach young kids discipline which then bred self-discipline, leadership skills, and how to have organized practices.

Because of the win-at-any-costs coaching mentality, young athletes aren't being taught discipline, which then teaches how-to **have the self-discipline to turn the performance facet on and off**.

There are consequences at the next level for "running" up the score...or "pimping" a home-run...or crowding the plate because you haven't developed the ability to hit an outside pitch to the opposite field.

We're going to go over a **simple fool-proof strategy** you can implement today in the following pages.

No OFFICIAL Standardized Youth Baseball/Softball Coaching Certification

Now, by the time you're reading this, this may have changed, but...

As I mentioned earlier, baseball and softball are low-entry coaching sports. Doesn't it bother you that the guy with meth-face, standing on the corner, and asking for a handout can coach your kids' team?

Now that may be a little extreme, but this fact alone should upset you! EXTREME LOW STANDARDS.

There's little to no fee to pay to be a baseball or softball coach...little to no certification process you have to sit through to **gain the knowledge to be effective**...and certainly no disciplinary action taken with subpar coaches.

This is probably why when young athletes get burned out of putting up with the daddy-ball politics, lack of disciplined coaches, and no league accountability for coaches exercising poor emotional control on the field...athletes go play another sport.

I'd do the same. Soccer – generally speaking – has their stuff together. I had to **pay a fee and sit through a certification seminar** to coach 10U girls soccer back in the late 2000's.

AND, there were hefty penalties of losing your certification if you acted like a knuckle-head on the field. Referees have the freedom to issue red cards to coaches or parents for their lack of field composure and self-discipline. Enough of these cards and fines have to be paid.

Nowadays, with the sub-par field composure of some players and coaches in Little League, we could probably feed all the hungry in the US with the fines!

Here's another problem for new or even veteran coaches...

Where to Start Training

The biggest problem for a new *volunteer* parent, who maybe didn't have much time playing the game, is where to start in the development process on the diamond. In this book, we're going to give you the most critical starting point.

I took the liberty of asking the top 1% of coaches where they would start **if only four weeks to train before the Little League World Series.**

We'll get to that later, but for now let's close this Introduction Chapter with the last challenge new coaches face...

Building a Sticky Team Culture

Successful businesses do this all the time like Zappos, Apple, and Google. Building a team culture, or *"how we do things here"*, is a must! This creates a sense of future belonging, which attracts parents and athletes who WANT to be a part of something bigger and special.

Tapping into the scarcity principal (there's only room for "X" number of players on this team) is a very high motivator, and ignites a passion to play on your teams.

Don't worry, we're going to address all these coaching concerns in this book. The following information was created for those beginning baseball or softball coaches, and those coaching veterans looking to put the power of empirical research (principles) behind their methods.

I've split the book up into three sections:

1. **KNOWLEDGE** (How-To Teach, Doing Things Right, "Effectiveness"): equipping inexperienced coaches, parents, and organizational leaders on how to effectively run their associations and teams,
2. **LEARNING** (How they learn) – the science of successful learning, optimizing how young athletes acquire new skills, and maintaining a rich soil for learning, AND
3. **DEVELOPMENT** (What to teach, Doing the Right Things, "Efficiency"): training crucial fundamentals like playing catch, opposite field hitting, and throwing strikes and locating pitches.

Now, let's get started with *Section One: Knowledge – Effectively "Doing Things Right"*…

1

SECTION 1, CHAPTER 1

KNOWLEDGE

How This Section Will Work...

In the following pages, we're going to be **equipping inexperienced coaches, parents, and organizational leaders on how-to effectively run their teams**.

I asked thousands of my email subscribers what the two most frustrating things were about coaching Little League. Here are the common KNOWLEDGE-related frustrations coming from coaches, parents, and organizational leaders:

- Unpaid volunteers – coaches and org. leaders
- Poor quality officiating – at the youth level
- **Either too competitive, or "trophy for participation" driven – both extremes aren't healthy**
- No baseball/softball experience, uneducated, lack of preparation, traditional coaching methods with no research backing (pass down good ol' boy coaching)
- Lack of free coaching training at LittleLeague.org
- Uneducated parents coaching from the bleachers
- Daddy-ball politics and lack of responsibility for kids' long term development
- Intimidating, yelling, belittling
- Parent false expectations for kid's skill level

Do you subscribe to any of the hot button bullet points above? Many times you've probably heard these used as crutches or excuses. As a Sticky Coach you want to be proactive and NOT reactive.

As we dive into the following information, I want you to keep some of these points in mind. **I'll do my best to address** these common frustrations with what Science and the Top 1% of coaches say about them.

But first, I want to share with you one important piece to the effective coaching puzzle for building a team's sticky culture…it's based around Tony LaRussa's 2011 World Championship mantra of **EFFORT & EXECUTION**…

The Science Of Sticky Coaching Credo

- **Laying Bricks (& Tracking Results)**: Disciplined steady progress and improvement over time, and understanding development happens at different speeds
- **Wear your Horse-Blinders:** Motivation to execute a skill rather than win a game. Improve for the 'next level'
- **Come Prepared**: P*layers*: dressed and ready, water, snacks. *Coaches*: RAMP Warm-up, written practice plan with a purpose (Fail to prepare, plan to fail)
- **Game-Play:** Make practice FUN and Engaging
- **'Earn' your Black-belt**: Praising-for-effort. Welcome the struggle. Goals, Steps, and Reps
- **Realize FAILURE is a BIG Part of this Game**: Transference = training for life!
- **Operate at a Higher Level**: work on building Character rather than Reputation
- **Respect Authority**: coaches, umpires, yours and other parents, teammates, and opposing players
- **Mirrors, NOT Windows**: Look in the mirror rather than out the window…*"How can I improve in this moment?".* Accountability!
- **Control ONLY What You Can Control**: Attitude, Effort, and Concentration

These are now your team's Core Values. **Screen shot this** and pin it up where you'll most frequent it. Commit these ten points to memory, and even have parents and players do the same. This is the **first critical step to creating a sticky team culture**.

These will make running a team or organization more effective if you live by them every single day. They'll also help answer challenging moral or ethical questions on and off the field. And the best part is, they're based on empirical research and study!!

The Art of Effective Sticky Coaching

Imagine doing a wild African tour of the Serengeti…your guide? An elephant…your brain…and a path. About the Serengeti, according to Wikipedia:

> *"Approximately 70 larger mammals and some 500 avifauna species are found there. This high diversity in terms of species is a function of diverse habitats ranging from riverine forests, swamps, kopjes, grasslands and woodlands. Currently there is* **controversy surrounding a proposed road** *that is to be built through the Serengeti."*

When I think of the Serengeti, I think desert. But it actually supports many kinds of environmental habitats. And what I found interesting, especially for the *Art of Effective Sticky Coaching* section, was the idea of a proposed path through it.

In their groundbreaking book, *Switch: How To Change Things When Change Is Hard*, Chip and Dan Heath create a metaphor **for change and building healthy habits.** We will be revisiting this metaphor throughout the Course.

Remember the guides I first introduced you to on your tour through the Serengeti? Here's how the Heath brothers' metaphor shakes out…

- **The Rider** ("your brain") – Goal setting, future planning, and organization.
- **The Elephant** – Emotional drive to take action, aka motivation.

- **Shaping the Path** – The controversial proposed road through the Serengeti

Chip and Dan Heath explain it like this…

If the Rider (goal planning) knows where he wants to go, but the elephant (emotion) doesn't have the motivation – or inspiration – to go anywhere, then the Rider is stuck. Think of this as working out or learning something new by reading a non-fiction book. most of the time, they're important non-urgent tasks that we tend to put off…the elephant isn't inspired or motivated enough.

Or, if the elephant is motivated to move, but the Rider keeps telling it *"STOP! You're going the wrong way!"* then again, the Rider is stuck **going to the middle of nowhere**. Think of the emotional power of a craving to eat sugary foods when you're mentally drained.

OR, if the Rider and Elephant are on the same page, but have no clear path, then they're both stuck.

See the dilemma here? As with coaching…

Sometimes it's a preparedness issue with the coach (The Rider). Sometimes it's **motivating and inspiring young athletes to follow through** with their practice at home (The Elephant). Sometimes we just don't know the right direction to go (Shaping the Path). Knowing the Goal…Steps…and Reps.

The information throughout the book will be broken up into "Guiding the Rider", "Motivating the Elephant", and "Shaping the Path."

2

SECTION 1, CHAPTER 2

KNOWLEDGE: Guiding The Rider

Become Top 5% in Little League Coaches in 6-12 Months...

In this section, we're going to cover what Tim Ferriss, author of the NY Times Best Selling book *The Four Hour Chef*, says about meta-learning:

- *What* you study is more important than *how* you study,
- Principles: Highest frequency **material that transfers** to everything, and
- Effectiveness is doing the right things.

What you study is more important than *how* you study

People get so numb watching millions of hours of slow motion hitting footage, that they lose sight of the forest for the trees. **They don't focus on the big picture principles, and doing the right things.**

First of all, don't spend hours and hours looking at big-guys like Josh Hamilton and Albert Pujols. If anyone is going to get away with ineffective mechanics, they are.

Then what do you study?

We must look through a filtered lens with specified criteria for evaluating key performance models. In hitting, what I do is look at the smaller guys hitting like bigger guys. Guys like Jose Bautista, Andrew McCutchen, Dustin Pedroia, Robinson Cano, and David Wright. **They HAVE to do things right** to compete! This is where *what* you study is more important than *how* you study.

What do these small power guys all have in common?

Principles: high frequency material that transfers to everything

There are certain things – bio-mechanically speaking – that small power hitters are consistently doing well. Like creating pre-swing torque in the shoulder-spine-hip combo, setting up in a strong versus weak position, and un-weighting the bat with a body's center of mass.

The test is to see if **these principles show up frequently in** other explosive rotational athletes, such as:

- Olympic Shot Putters,
- Discus Throwers,
- Golfers, and
- Lacrosse players.

AND WE DO! Sure, each athletic movement "gets it done" a little differently, but one thing's for sure, these athletes are ALL adhering to the same human movement rules or principles.

These principles are like the bumpers in the gutters hugging the lane at a bowling alley. I don't care what path the ball takes down the lane, just as long as it stays between the bumpers.

Albert Einstein was always striving for finding the high frequency material that transferred to everything in his search for simplifying his Theory of Relativity. He was always **seeking the commandments of the universe**, looking for what materials overlapped with other scientific disciplines.

That's what this book has found for you.

Effectiveness is doing the right things

Instead of solely looking at what baseball or softball coaches are doing right, we need to force ourselves outside the sport and study how other coaching and teaching principles are being effective, and can possibly apply to other sports.

We need to **find common ground**…where all the circles intersect, if you will.

Not only that, but we have to look at what neuroscience, bio-chemistry, biology, and psychology say about how the brain effectively absorbs information. What are the principles that are validated by Science that overwhelmingly agree with coaching high level athletes?

Remember, us humans have been around for a long time, and **our behaviors haven't changed**. There are biological and psychological human principles that are at work today like they were hundreds of thousands of years ago. Our goal in this book is to find them.

Remember, in this section we studied:

- *What* you study is more important than *how* you study,
- Principles: Highest frequency material that transfers to everything, and
- Effectiveness is doing the right things.

3

SECTION 1, CHAPTER 3

KNOWLEDGE: Guiding The Rider

How-To Make Coaching Sticky (Three Simple Secrets)

In this section, we're going to discuss:

- Teaching detailed fundamentals using "trained eyes",
- Take time out for a teaching moment, and
- Relentless teaching follow-through.

Teaching detailed fundamentals using "trained eyes"

Have you ever bought a new car and noticed that once you drove it off the lot that everywhere you looked, everyone and their mother seemed to be driving the same vehicle?

Your **eyes have been trained** to see that new car. The technical term for this is your Reticular Activating System.

You've experienced "trained eyes" if you've bought a particular piece of clothing, gone to where a ton of people are, and spot that same piece on a few others.

The same "trained eyes" can be used by a Marine sniper hiding in combat looking for a specific 'target'.

On slow motion analysis video, I'm looking for different things like setup, head positioning, footwork, and spine driven movement mechanics. I've trained my eyes to look for these things.

This is how the brain is able to focus and concentrate on a given task, and it's how us coaches should operate as well. And by working at it, your brain will get faster and more efficient at doing this.

Later, in the DEVELOPMENT Section, you'll learn which fundamentals to teach and what mistakes to look for to engage what top coaches call…

The "teaching moment"

In Daniel Coyle's book *The Talent Code*, he speaks of a teacher named Skye Carmen at Meadowmount Music School in Westport, New York. They're top-of-the-line when it comes to developing fantastic music students.

Mrs. Skye credits the school's notoriety to consistently taking a timeout for the "teaching moment". It's when a mistake is made, maybe a bad musical note, and the teacher stops the class to correct the mistake.

Skye talks about how **it's not how fast you can do it, but how slow you can do it right**.

Skye says,

> *"Learn to feel it...if you hear a string out of tune, it should bother you...it should bother you a lot. That's what you need to feel...**it's concentration, and that's what we need to practice, feeling.**"*

Oftentimes, getting the hitter to feel something different or awkward is the key. If it feels awkward, then they're doing something different. As the new movement is refined through repetition, then awkward moves into comfortable. As Tony Robbins says,

> *"Repetition is the mother of skill."*

Skye has a proven four-step process for learning:

1. Pick a target,
2. Reach for it,
3. Evaluate the gap between the target and the reach, and
4. Return to step one.

As a coach, if a player doesn't execute a skill correctly, then **stop practice**, and initiate the teaching moment. Get into the habit of following the four above steps.

Aside from a teaching moment, here's another critical ingredient that doesn't get much air-time...

Relentless teaching follow-through

Legendary Coach Bob Bennett would frustrate my teammates and I when engaging in a "teaching moment" when we were playing baseball at Fresno State.

He wouldn't leave us alone **until we finally executed the skill correctly** from start to finish. Back then I hated it, but now as a full time instructor I really do appreciate his follow through. I use this with my students.

You see, when I interviewed Coach Bennett recently for this book, he used an analogy for relentless teaching follow through. He said it'd be like a History teacher talking about former President Abraham Lincoln during a lecture. Then a student's hand pops up to make a comment...

Student: *"Teacher, I just watched a movie that said Abraham Lincoln was a vampire killer."*
Teacher: *"No, I'm sorry Johnny, the movie is fictional."*
Student: *"Teacher, someone on Facebook confirmed President Lincoln was a vampire killer."*
Teacher: *"No Johnny, I'm sorry that's not true."*
Student: *"Teacher, my dog said Abraham Lincoln was a vampire killer"*
Teacher: *"Okay...? Moving on..."*

Oftentimes, this is what happens to a player who – after a teaching moment – continues making a bad throw to first base, and the coach let's 'it' go to just continue on with practice.

This can't happen and is negligent for proper development. A coach has to take a timeout and follow through on their teaching. Even if they have to regress the player – or team!! – for a moment, until they get it right.

Remember, in this section, you learned:

- How-to teach detailed fundamentals using "trained eyes",
- To take time out for a teaching moment, and
- How crucial relentless teaching follow-through is.

Next, I want to show you how-to to keep the team focused on the most urgent things…

4

SECTION 1, CHAPTER 4

KNOWLEDGE: Guiding The Rider

Why I Ask This Question (and maybe you should too)

In this section, we'll be discussing:

- *Possibility Thinking*, by Robert Schuller,
- "What's the real issue?", and
- Playing pepper as an example.

"Possibility Thinking"

Coach Bob Bennett highly recommended to me Robert H. Schuller's book *Possibility Thinking: If It's Going To Be, It's Up To Me*.

In the book, there was a story of someone wanting to build a church. They first focused on rounding up contractors willing to donate their time to the cause. The church visionary had difficulty getting anyone to just donate their time.

The first failed attempt at starting the church construction forced the visionaries to ask the question, **"what's the real issue here?"** Contractors didn't want to donate their time because it takes them away from the more desirable paid-time work. So, money was the real issue.

With this new focus, concentration went away from finding contractors, to raising the money needed to hire the contractors.

We're going to be using a baseball example shortly, but first…

"What's the real issue?"

Think of a baseball or softball team as:

1. A) Coach = Visionary (CEO), and
2. B) Players = Management.

If you had to get through a dense jungle, the visionaries are the ones who climb to the top of the tree to get the big picture of where to lead the team, while management uses their machete to cut the dense foliage down, so they can see what's right in front of them.

I coach's job is to troubleshoot what the real issue is, and where he wants the team's focus to be – it takes a visionary to do this. It's not rocket science either. Don't waste time being negative about your players NOT executing their deep cutoffs well, and then moving on with practice as usual. Take a timeout for a teaching moment.

Here's a bad model of NOT using *Possibility Thinking*...

I just witnessed a father and his son out hitting in the cage next to me. The dad was throwing batting practice to his seven-year-old pride and joy. Unfortunately, the son kept stopping his bat at contact. Instead of the Dad being a visionary, he tried cutting down the braches in front of his face by yelling at his son, "WHY DO YOU KEEP DOING THAT!!?" Whereas the son sadly replied, "I don't know dad."

Here's a good model of *Possibility Thinking* in action...

The game of Pepper as an example

In case you didn't know already...what is Pepper? According to Wikipedia,

> "Pepper is a common pre-game exercise where one player hits brisk grounders and line drives to a group of fielders who are standing around twenty feet away. The fielders throw to the batter who uses a short, light swing to hit the ball on the ground back towards the fielders. The fielders field the ground balls and continue tossing the ball to the batter. **This exercise keeps the fielders and batter alert, and helps to develop quickness and good hand-eye coordination.**"

If you're having your athletes play Pepper, and the observation resembles a Ringling Brothers Barnum & Bailey Circus Show, then as a coach, use Schuller's *Possibility Thinking*...what's the real issue here?

If the fielders are having trouble throwing strikes to the hitters, then a teaching moment must be taken. **The focus will indefinitely be regressed to playing catch, "belt-to-hat".**

You would start them at a shorter distance, and once they're ninety-percent accurate there, then progressively stretch the player-pairs until you get them to the desired Pepper distance. To make throwing strikes more challenging for the fielders, move the fielders back ten feet.

Pepper can also be included in the practice schedule as "Game-Play", which we'll be introducing later in this book.

Remember, in this section, we covered:

- *Possibility Thinking*, by Robert Schuller,
- "What's the real issue?", and
- Playing pepper as an example.

The next section will make the act of coaching ten-times easier...

5

SECTION 1, CHAPTER 5

KNOWLEDGE: Guiding The Rider

What Players are Eagerly Looking for in Coaches

In this section, we'll be learning how-to:

- Write detailed practices anyone can follow,
- Eliminate filler time, and
- Skill-oriented condition and RAMP warm-ups.

How-to write detailed practices anyone can follow

I've mentioned the following quote earlier, *"If you fail to plan, then you plan to fail"*. You left-brained thinkers embrace this, while right-brained people hate it. Writing out a practice plan in advance will make the art of sticky coaching much easier for coaches, players, and parents involved.

The idea here is to **think ahead and put down on paper what your team's focus is going to be for practices**. This will empower assistant coaches, players, and innocent bystander parents to have the ability to help execute an effective practice.

The key is to follow the paper practice plan to the letter, and NOT just putting it down on paper, and then "winging it".

The Top 1% of coaches all do this. At Fresno State, we players could always expect Coach Bob Bennett to have the practice plan posted by noon, so that we could see what we were going to be working on.

He even saved old practice plans with notes on what worked and what didn't. Yes it takes extra work to do this, and yes you're probably only an unpaid volunteer coach, but **planning and tracking your practices will definitely give you – and everyone else – peace of mind**.

Even John Wooden, ten-time UCLA national championship basketball coach, did this. It takes more work that first year, but with your saved written practice plans and notes, the next year will flow much better.

You see, **players are eagerly looking for their coaches to be organized, and know what the heck

they're doing (being a visionary). You know how it feels to be on vacation in big confusing city like San Francisco, following a caravan of cars, and finding out the people you're following, don't know where the heck they're going.

Like Coach Bennett says, in his *The Complete Book of Baseball Handouts* (http://gohpl.com/bbennettcombook), posting a schedule does FOUR things:

1. Notifies players, trainers, and coaching staff
2. Promotes organization
3. **Promotes common-language terminology**
4. Encourages pre-planning by players.

Here are the benefits of having a posted schedule and encouraging athletes to practice without a coach:

- Teaches responsibility to follow the practice schedule and each player's own schedule.
- Encourages players to make their own practice session.
- Points up the fallacy of the statement, *"there's nothing to work on the last month of the season"*.
- Reinforces the fact that **each player's refinements and challenges are never completed**.

Now keep in mind, Coach Bennett is speaking about young adult college kids with driver's licenses and living away from home. A Little League coach can't just sit below in the clubhouse during practices. But, a Sticky Coach can post a practice schedule, and then be a passive observer to see how the kids do running their own practice.

The following free PDF's were sampled from *The Complete Book of Baseball Handouts* linked to Amazon above:

- **Coach Bennett Practice Template #1** (http://gohpl.com/bbennettho1), includes:
    o Handout #116: Off-Season Guidelines
    o Handout #117: Fresno State Baseball—**Thursday Practice**
    o Handout #118: Fresno State Baseball—**Wednesday Practice**
- **Coach Bennett Practice Template #2** (http://gohpl.com/bbennettho2):
    o Handout #119: Fresno State Baseball—**Monday Practice** (intra-squad day)
    o Handout #120: Fresno State Baseball—Individual Practice Evaluation
    o Handout #121: Fresno State Baseball—Player Teammate Evaluation

You'll get to see specific drills to use in Module 3: DEVELOPMENT, but the basic recipe Coach Bennett uses is that in every practice, a coach should have scheduled:

1. **Playing catch** (this includes pitchers throwing their bullpens),
2. **Base-running**, and
3. **Defensive situations**.

Playing catch (defense), pitchers locating pitches, and proper base running.

As you'll find in the preceding PDF practice templates, you won't be able to practice everything on the template. Heck, you may not even know what some of the drills are. That's okay, for now, I just want you to see how a winning practice is organized.

And according to Coach Bob Bennett, one of the biggest mistakes coaches do is NOT...

Eliminating filler time

This is when players are standing or sitting around, being nonproductive, and not doing anything. **Filler time makes practices drag on, and doesn't make for very effective time management**. This is how players lose interest, and how the elephant (emotion) gets bored and demotivated or uninspired. These practices are definitely fly-by-the-seat-of-your-pants.

Otherwise, effective time managed practices would look something like this…

(Please refer to the Coach Bennett Practice Template #1 PDF above)

During batting practice:

- Pitchers – throw bullpens
- Pitchers – practice holding runners (big field)
- **Base-runners** – practicing leads (big field)
- Outfielders – fly balls
- Infielders – groundballs

Now, of course a Little League team may not be able to do all of this in one batting practice with only fourteen players, but I want you to notice how there's zero filler time.

Here's another example using the batting practice scenario…

When Coach Bennett managed Team USA in 1977 and 1979, he noticed Japan was doing something different than most teams during batting practice with their outfielders…

Instead of scattering pitchers and outfielders all throughout the outfield to shag balls, Japan had an organized line of players at each outfield position. One guy was "hot", and the others were standing behind him. Once the "hot" player got a ground/fly ball, then the next player stepped up for his turn.

A coach can do this in the infield as well…in addition to hitting fungo ground-balls to infielders in-between batted BP balls.

After Coach Bennett witnessed 'Japanese Baseball', Fresno State emulated this ever since. This brought a purpose to every player involved in batting practice.

Also notable to mention about base-running during batting practice, that when a hitter finishes their "round" of batting practice, they sprint down to first base like they're beating out an infield single. Then from there the base-runner could practice leads, stealing, and hit and running to second. Then on second, he could practice getting a great secondary lead and anticipating a ball in the dirt, stealing third, or seeing the ball through on the left side of the diamond. At third, the base-runner could practice anticipating a ball in the dirt, and tagging on a fly ball.

This will put 'eliminating filler time' on steroids.

You don't have enough coaches? That's why you have a practice plan written down, so **any bystander parents can read it and have a clue of how to help**. Posting the practice plan in-between your ears doesn't help anyone.

Heck, even high motivation, high skilled players *(you'll learn more about this tactic later)* can help out. Get everyone involved! The more "trained eyes" the better.

Again, put thought and purpose into each practice. Because you'll be asking for the same focused effort and concentration from your players.

FYI, **most of the time, LIVE games will determine what your focus at practice will be**. I know that whenever a fly ball was dropped in-between the 'Bermuda triangle' at Fresno State during a game – between two outfielders and a middle infielder – we all expected to see PFP's (Pop-Fly Priorities) on the next practice day (See *Coach Bennett Practice Template #1, Handout #118—Wednesday Practice*).

These were the worst sprint intervals you could ever do. With two to three outfielders spread out between three stations, Coach Bennett hitting 'tweener' pop-flies in rapid succession, and after twenty to thirty minutes of PFP's, a few of us were puking!

Initiate skill-oriented conditioning and RAMP warm-ups

Coach Bennett, in our interview, **was adamant about using skill oriented conditioning whenever possible**. In other words, base running instead of wind sprints. Not that wind sprints are bad…you're just killing two birds with one stone when you have players sprinting home to first, and legging out doubles, triples, and inside-the-park homers.

Typically, whenever the infielders needed base runners, guess whose job it was to get into run downs, steal bases, and leg out first-to-third hit and runs? Us outfielders and 'non-athlete' pitchers, that's who! We all thought we were track stars by the end of the season.

Another good conditioning exercise Coach Bennett would do with the outfielders and pitchers was he'd hit us fungo post-routes, football-style. He was VERY good with the fungo by the way. **He'd hit the ball just beyond our reach, urging us to sprint harder next time**.

Coach Bennett says to only use wind sprints and medium distance sprinting (one-minute walls and foul poles) as punishment.

Minute-walls are when you have all players line up on the left field foul line and give them a minute to run to center field and back (on the big field). Once the minute is up, do it all over again. For example, we had one guy show up late to 6:30am weights one morning, and we ALL watched the sun come up running over thirty minute-walls *(it was more than that, but we all lost count after thirty)*.

And, Foul Poles are when you split players up three at a time, line them up on the left field foul line warning track (or near the fence), and have them run full or progressive timed sprints. These sucked too, but were effective. After they pitch, you also see pitchers running these at a slower pace as a recovery tool.

PLEASE NOTE: **with younger Little Leaguers, you never want to punish them with running**. Their first experiences with conditioning need to be constructive and fun (or even competitive). This has to do with psychological anchoring, which is another book for another day.

RAMP warm-ups

To begin practice, you'll want to use a RAMP warm-up. RAMP stands for:

- **R**ange-of-motion
- **A**ctivation
- **M**ovement **P**reparation

Usually, this will consist of some quick mobility and stability exercises for the ankles, hips, mid-back, shoulders, and core. If you've ever watched the MLB Network channel, when they visit the different ballparks during pre-game warm-ups, then you'll probably see players warming up with long colorful resistance bands. They're doing a RAMP warm-up.

Below is a sample RAMP I do with my beginning hitters:

1. RAMP Beginner – http://gohpl.com/rampbeginners
2. Here's an HPL blog post with a buffet of dynamic warm-up exercise videos: http://gohpl.com/bbfpwarmup

We just went over the **elements players are eagerly looking for in a coach**. Remember, we went over how-to:

- Write detailed practices anyone can follow,
- Eliminate filler time, and
- Initiate skill-oriented conditioning and RAMP warm-ups.

6

SECTION 1, CHAPTER 6

KNOWLEDGE: Guiding The Rider

Focus on ONLY These Two Things...

In this section, we'll be looking at:

- If you ONLY had 4-weeks to train for the LLWS,
- If you ONLY had 8-weeks to train for the LLWS, and
- The difference between fine and rough coaching eyes.

In my interview with Team Avenue's Thomari Story-Harden, and Coach Bob Bennett, I asked them:

> *"If you were to train me for four weeks for the Little League World Series and had a million dollars on the line, what would the training look like?"*

And then I added,

> *"What if I trained for eight weeks?"*

Before I get into practice application, I wanted to mention something really important that my friend Thomari, founder of Team Avenue, said in our interview. That it's really important for a coach to **identify the identity of the team**.

What's this mean?

Do you have a group of young athletes who can really mash the ball? Or do you have smaller ones you'll be going station-to-station with (hit-and-run, bunt, and stealing).

This is critical, because although you can maximize consistent power with each hitter no matter what their size, you still can't make a guy like Dustin Pedroia hit over forty bombs a season. Surely, he'll average 44 doubles per season, but he's a station to station type player.

So, keep this in mind, as you **formulate the vision and purpose of each team you coach**. And if you coach the same team for the next five years, you may have to identify which kind of team you'll be working with from year to year, because the kids are still growing and developing.

If only had 4-weeks to train for LLWS?

After the last word of the question left my mouth, there wasn't a moment's hesitation when Coach Bennett blurted out pitching and defense.

For pitchers...throwing strikes (*I would also add pitch location into this formula*). For defense...playing catch.

Notice how with pitching, Coach didn't say, develop a curve-ball, slider, slerve, spit, knuckle-ball, or "terminator" pitch (*poor reference to the movie Major League 2*)? His answer was simple, throw strikes. We've all heard the saying, *"Great pitching stops great hitting"*.

Now, onto defense...

I was told recently by one of my online parents that 90% of plays in Little League *should* be an out at first base. Notice the word *'should'* in there. There's a big reason why most Little League coaches want their kids hitting the ball on the ground...because **they know most kids at that level don't know how to play catch**. With a majority of teams, a ground-ball is a hit over fifty percent of the time in Little League because the defense can't play catch.

You see, three things have to take place to successfully field and throw a batted ground-ball:

1. Field the ball,
2. Throw the ball, and
3. The receiver catches the ball.

In catching a fly ball, there's only one: catch it. And that's why some pro ground-ball hitting coaches say you can't get a "bad hop" in the air. But this thinking is flawed. WHY? What's one of the golden pitching rules? To keep the ball down in the zone. As a result, what part of the ball do pitchers want hitters hitting? The top half – to increase the amount of "worm burners" the defense can convert. If we're teaching our hitters to do the same, then aren't we just feeding into what the pitchers want hitters doing?!

In addition, **coaching 12u hitters to hit the ball on the ground is short-sighted and a part of the "winning!" mentality**. When these squads play better teams, the hogs (the greedy) and lambs (the naïve) will get slaughtered.

If only had 8-weeks to train

When I gave Coach Bennett a little more slack and told him he now has eight weeks to train me, he said he'd still focus on pitchers throwing strikes, and fielders being able to play catch, but with one small twist...he'd increase the level of difficulty.

To put it another way, **he'd push his players' limits**.

This could be cut-offs, Pepper, double plays, hit and runs, stretching out a fielder's five-dimensional range, pitchers around the infield, bunt plays, run-downs, etc.

In the DEVELOPMENT Module, we'll be going over how to shrink the game down, to get more quality repetitions in, but for now with a truncated coaching schedule, Coach Bennett explained the importance of...

Fine and rough coaching eyes

Fine coaching eyes are for the players who're highly skilled. With these types of players, a coach has to train their eyes to see small blemish details. It could be the way a shortstop plants with his back foot with a ground ball in the six-hole…It could be getting a hitter to relax the jaw muscles during impact to keep from over-swinging…It could be a pitcher's unstable landing foot.

I like to use video analysis when coaching with fine eyes. Sometimes fine details are hard to spot in real time.

Rough coaching eyes are for players who are less skilled. You can forgive the small mistakes, but bigger ones not so much. Playing catch "belt-to-hat" is a rough eye detail, meaning throws have to make it between the receiving player's belt and hat. Making sure a hitter is un-weighting the bat by getting forward momentum, is a rough eye detail. Pitchers falling off the mound towards their glove side, is a rough eye detail.

As you'll find out later in the book, **playing detective and knowing your players is a critical element to great coaches**.

Remember, in this section, we went over:

- If you ONLY had 4-weeks to train for the LLWS,
- If you ONLY had 8-weeks to train for the LLWS, and
- The difference between fine and rough coaching eyes.

What you'll be reading next is where coaching and parenting start to intersect…

7

SECTION 1, CHAPTER 7

KNOWLEDGE: Guiding The Rider

"This Will Make a Coward Out of You"

It will because this is NOT the easy road to take. Nobody said volunteer coaching would be easy and simple. It can be a test of wills, and **can be as humbling as** walking out the door not knowing your fly is unzipped. Don't worry, with a little elbow grease, you'll be making the right strides before you know it. In this section, we'll be discussing:

- The importance of Discipline and Organization over skill development,
- How-to train kids to be leaders, and
- Kids as independent thinkers & problem solvers.

Importance of Discipline and Organization over skill development

What I mean is discipline and organization should be a prerequisite to skill development.
According to Daniel Coyle's book, *The Talent Code,*

> *"**Discipline is an early predictor of high IQ.** In a 2005 study, psychologists Martin Seligman and Angela Duckworth studied several parameters of 164 eighth graders, including IQ, along with five tests measuring self-discipline."*

Result?
Self-discipline was twice as accurate as IQ in predicting a students' GPA.
Legendary coach Bob Bennett told me about one of the most influential figures in his baseball life having one of the most profound effects on all that he's accomplished.
He talked about a man by the name of Damon Bailey. Don't worry, you've probably never heard of him in baseball or softball circles. Surprisingly, and according to Coach Bennett, **he didn't know diddly-squat about baseball, but he did know how** to enforce organized practices and sink self-discipline into kids.

By self-discipline, we mean building healthy habits and sticking to them.

The other thing Mr. Bailey was good at was he knew about kids and what they wanted to get out of life. And he ultimately did what he could to make them leaders.

Having a plan and a purpose every meeting can have such a lasting effect on small minds. **It's not the baseball or softball skills that will help them succeed in life**…it's teaching self-discipline and the organizational know-how that'll make them leaders.

How-to train kids to be leaders

Here are a couple bullet points from St. Louis Cardinals' Coach Mike Matheny's Letter to Parents…

"It's ALL about the boys:

- *To teach these young men how to play the game of baseball the right way,*
- *To be a positive impact on them as young men, and*
- *Do all of this with class.*

Players perform with Class (character), Respect others (coaches, umpires, parents, and players), **be Accountable for actions***, come prepared to play, and practice Self-Discipline."*

There's a word that can sum up this section of Coach Matheny's Letter, and it's called Transference. According to the Merriam-Webster Dictionary, Transference means:

1: an act, process, or instance of transferring: conveyance, transfer

2: **the redirection of feelings and desires and especially of those unconsciously retained from childhood toward a new object** (as a psychoanalyst conducting therapy)

In other words, as a coach, teaching young athletes how to think and act in a way that will transfer to other areas of their life. Whether you like it or not coaches, you're a life coach! Our job is to make leaders out of young men and women.

Kids as independent thinkers & problem solvers

A man by the name of Thomas Carruthers once said,

"A teacher is one who makes himself progressively unnecessary."

I couldn't agree more. St. Louis Cardinals baseball Coach Mike Matheny also put in his Letter to Parents, about the importance of teaching young athletes a thought process.

He stresses to his players to **have a purpose for doing things on the field**. And this was something echoed to me by Coach Bennett when I played for him.

Here's the question that was often asked of me after a questionable decision I made:

"What were you thinking?"

Such as, what was I thinking in the outfield when I threw the ball to third instead of second – with one out – and a hit and run on, instead of throwing to second to keep the double play in order. Or, what was I thinking sacrificing a bunt down the third base line with a runner on first instead of down the first base line and making their defense work harder to field and throw to first.

'What were you thinking?' MUST be asked in a constructive way…in a way Coach was trying to get at my thought process…or lack thereof. Asking this question over and over, conditions players to ask this of themselves before a play even occurs.

A player has to learn how-to role-play and weigh the probabilities of near future situations before they come up, so they can be prepared for whatever happens.

Mike Batesole, head baseball coach to the 2008 Fresno State Bulldogs College World Series Champions – and whom I played for in 2003 – calls this a "think ahead."

Remember, it's definitely a challenge for a coach to:

- Focus on Discipline and Organization rather than skill development (at first),
- Train kids to be leaders, and
- Build a thought process for young players to be independent thinkers & problem solvers.

This will make a coward out of any coach, especially a volunteer coach. This requires A LOT of extra work and energy, and takes a developmental mentality. **You're not just a baseball or softball coach. You're a life coach.** Understood?

8

SECTION 1, CHAPTER 8

KNOWLEDGE: Guiding The Rider

John Wooden's TEN Key Coaching Commandments

In "Part Three: Master Coaching", of Daniel Coyle's book *The Talent Code*, purely observational LIVE research of John Wooden by academics Gallimore and Tharp suggested ten key commandments:

> 1. 75% of Wooden's acts of teaching (2,326 total tallied) were pure information: **what to do, how to do it, when to intensify an activity**.
> 2. **He modeled the right way to do it, showed the incorrect way, and then remodeled the right way.** *[I call this the right-way sandwich]*
> 3. Coach would spend two hours each morning with his assistants planning that day's practice, then write out the minute-by-minute schedule on 3X5 cards. He kept cards from year to year, so he could compare and adjust.
> 4. What made Wooden a great coach wasn't praise, wasn't denunciation, and certainly wasn't pep talks. It was the Gatling-gun rattle of targeted information he fired at his players. This, not that. Here, not there.
> 5. Laws of learning: **explanation, demonstration, imitation, correction, and repetition.** This would look like: me explaining a specific skill movement, me showing them the movement, the player imitating me, I correct them, and continue the process.
> 6. Seek small improvement, one day at a time…don't seek the big improvements.
> 7. Error-centered, well planned, information-rich practices.
> 8. Talk in short imperative bursts.
> 9. *"Study the way young people react, the way they're motivated, the way they're frustrated, and when I discover that, I'm halfway there."* – Wooden
> 10. **Great coaches are the product of** research, planning, continuous improvement, subject mastery, effective teaching (the art of), and a dedicated teacher.

This information alone has taken my instructing to another level. Do you understand how dialed in – as a coach – you have to be to win ten NCAA championships with one school in twelve years (1963-75)?!

Another thing researchers Gallimore and Tharp mentioned – from their research observing Wooden – was that **people practice too much**. We have to get movement to sink into the brain, not the body. Visualization is where crucial connections are made. The body doesn't know the difference of whether you're working out repetitions in your mind or on the field.

We're going to dig into this more during *Module Three: DEVELOPMENT* when we talk about shrinking the game down. Physical reps don't make coaching stick, mental reps do! It's all about deeper practice. The brain MUST work and struggle with new things, that's how we learn and get better.

Also, you can **search in Google Images for the "john wooden pyramid of success"**, screenshot it or print out, and save.

Remember, in this section, we kept it simple and analyzed:

- John Wooden's TEN key coaching commandments

9

SECTION 1, CHAPTER 9

KNOWLEDGE: Guiding The Rider

Best Diplomatic Ways for Policing Parents (the up-front agreement)

In this section, we'll be going over two important bits of information:

- Psychology of Hyper-Parenting,
- Parent Pledge PDF

Psychology of Hyper-Parenting

There are four types of over-achieving parents, according to the book *Brain Rules for Baby*, by John Medina:

1. **Gourmet parents**: these parents are high achievers who want their kids to succeed as they did.
2. **College-degree parents**: your classic "hot-housers", these parents are related to Gourmets but believe that the sooner academic training starts, the better.
3. **Outward-bound parents**: wanting to provide their kids with physical survival skills because the world is such a dangerous place, their parents are often involved in the military and law enforcement.
4. **Prodigy parents**: financially successful and deeply suspicious about the education system, their parents want to guard their kids against the negative effects of schooling.

Losing or not having control over a still-developing human being is a difficult paradigm to shift for some. John Medina also says in the book that hyper-parenting hurts a child's intellectual development for three reasons:

#1: Extreme expectations stunt higher-level thinking: If little kids sense a parent wants them to accomplish some intellectual feat for which their brains are not yet ready, they are inexorably forced into a corner. This coerces the brain to revert to "lower-level" thinking strategies, creating counterfeit habits that may have to be unlearned later. For example, memorization versus understanding a concept ("pony tricks")

#2: Pressure can extinguish curiosity: kids are natural explorers (or scientists). If a parent supplies rigid educational expectations, interests are transformed into appeasements. Kids stop asking potent questions like *"Am I curious about this?"* and start asking *"What will satisfy the powers at be?"* Exploratory behavior is not rewarded, so then it's disregarded. Brain is a survival organism, and there's nothing more important than safety (approval in this case) the parent can provide.

#3: Continual anger or disappointment becomes toxic stress: these are the pushy, demanding, and obnoxious parents we all know. This leads to "learned helplessness," for example, a kid comes home to a drunken father who beats him…the kid needs a home, but it's awful to be at home. This leads to a failure to live up to parents' expectations. The brain is not interested in learning…its interest is in survival. Parenting is NOT a race. Kids are not proxies for adult success.

Yes I know John Medina is talking about parenting here, but remember when I said teaching, coaching, and parenting run along the same highway.

Parent Pledge PDF

To download the **Positive Coaching Alliance's** Parent Pledge PDF click the following link:
http://gohpl.com/pcaparentpledge

Positive Coaching Alliance (PCA) is a national non-profit developing "Better Athletes, Better People" by working to provide all youth and high school athletes a positive, character-building youth sports experience. You can also CLICK the following link to watch a nine-minute mini-documentary YouTube video about PCA:
http://gohpl.com/aboutpca

As a coach, you can send the Parent Pledge PDF to parents via email – or print out copies instead – and give them to your parents to sign and return to you.

In this section, we went over two important bits of information:

- Psychology of Hyper-Parenting, and
- Parent Pledge PDF (a Positive Coaching Alliance (PCA resource)

10

SECTION 1, CHAPTER 10

KNOWLEDGE: Motivating The Elephant

The #1 Way to Get Athletes to Listen You

In this section, we're to going to learn how-to appeal to a younger athlete by:

- Perfecting the Fine Art of Empathy,
- STEP 1: Describing what emotional changes you think you see, and
- STEP 2: Make a guess as to wear those emotional changes came from.

Remember, the quote by John Wooden in the ten key coaching commandments pulled from the Gallimore and Tharp study…

> *"**Study the way young people react**, the way they're motivated, the way they're frustrated, and when I discover that, I'm halfway there."* – John Wooden

Perfecting the Fine Art of Empathy

To take this one step further, let's look at Stephen R. Covey's number one bestselling book, *The 7 Habits of Highly Successful People*. In the book, Covey states…

> *"**Seek first to understand, then to be understood.**"*

This is habit number five in the book, and when I read this chapter in the late 2000's, it wrecked my life. It sounds so counter-intuitive, and it was (and still is) a difficult thought process for me to execute especially when I'm emotional.

Covey cites five levels of listening (from least to most effective):

1. **Ignoring** – not listening to the person at all.
2. **Pretending** – "Yeah. Uh-huh. Right."

3. **Selective Listening** – hearing only certain parts of the conversation. This is often done when listening to the constant chattering of a pre-school child.

4. **Attentive Listening** – paying attention and focusing energy on the words that are being said.

5. **Empathic Listening** – listening with the intent to understand. Not mimicking what the other person says by rearranging your response to their words like you would in Selective or Attentive Listening. We'll get to an example of this in a second...

Empathic listening is seeing the world the way the other person sees the world. We've all heard the saying, *"Walking a mile in their shoes"*. The bottom line is that you understand how they feel by using every sense God gave you to see the world through their eyes.

According to Covey, next to physical survival, **the next most important human need is psychological survival** – to be understood, to be affirmed, to be validated, to be appreciated.

Diagnose before you prescribe. Here's how you do it in two simple steps...

STEP 1: Describe what emotional changes you think you see

These two steps to empathy were beautifully simplified in John Medina's book *Brain Rules for Baby*. One of the reasons empathy works so well, is because **it does not require a solution**. It only requires understanding.

If an athlete comes to you with a red face – huffing and puffing – then take a stab at the emotion their revealing to you. Are they frustrated? Angry? Disappointed? Embarrassed? A mix of the four?

You're **making an educated guess** based on what you're experiencing through all senses. It's not psycho-analysis either. There's no right or wrong. Put your best guess out there. I'm sure the athlete will surely correct you if you're off-base.

Then there's the second step...

STEP 2: Make a guess as to wear those emotional changes came from

We'll use the above player for example,

Player: *(Comes off the field red-faced and huffy-puffy).*
Coach: *"You look frustrated..."*
Player: *"Uh-huh."*
Coach: *"I know you're frustrated after bobbling the ball because you feel like you let the team down putting that runner on."* (That eventually scored)
Player: *"Yeah, how stupid of me."*
Coach: *"What could you of done differently?"*
Player: *"Um, maybe I didn't mentally prepare before the pitch. That caused me to throw the ball before catching it first."*
Coach: *"That's okay, I know how you feel. At least next time, you'll know what you need to do."*

Most of the time, coaches go into prescribing before seeing the botched play through the players' eyes. The coach guides the player to the solution instead of giving him the solution. Remember, "Teach a man to fish..."?

I know when coaches prescribed to me right away; I felt my defense mechanism go up…I felt like they were harping and nagging me, versus **seizing the teaching moment**.

When I work with my hitting students I pay special close attention to when they're getting frustrated or mentally drained and why. This happens quite often because I don't let them get away with bad form and posture. I test them about what we just went over. I make their brain work. **I demand their attention, focus, and concentration during sessions.**

I make a conscience effort to check in with them when we're working together because the last thing I want to do is take them over the mental brink. I don't want them to completely fold like a lawn chair. And most importantly, I want them to come back! So, my antennae are up all the time. Checking in with what emotion they may be feeling and why.

Remember, in this section, we learned how-to appeal to a young athlete by:

- Perfecting the Fine Art of Empathy,
- Describing what emotional changes you think you see, and
- Make a guess as to wear those emotional changes came from.

Now, let's dive into…

11

SECTION 1, CHAPTER 11

KNOWLEDGE: Motivating The Elephant

FOUR-Virtues of Great Coaching

In this section, we're going to analyze the following great coaching ingredients:

1. **Knowledge,**
2. **Playing detective,**
3. **Communication,** and
4. **Theatrical honesty.**

We're getting ready to go into what Daniel Coyle talks about in his book *The Talent Code*...the LOVE of coaching. Coyle surveyed great fly-under-the-radar teachers and coaches, to find out what they all had in common. Here's what he discovered:

- They made initial learning very pleasant and rewarding.
- Made learning fun like a game.
- Gave positive reinforcement.
- Were rarely critical (negative) of child. And,
- Set standards, expecting child to make progress, and this was largely **done using approval and praise-for-effort**.

In other words,
   A great coach has good knowledge of the subject, can recognize errors, and can connect the student to the solution.
   Here are the definitions of Coyle's virtues of great coaching…

Virtue #1: Knowledge

Knowledge that is comprehensible to learners. Coaching knowledge in the form of technical knowledge, strategy, experience, and practiced instinct should be ready and able to be put to instant use by locating and understanding where the students are and where they need to go.

The coach may have once been a promising talent in their respective field, failed, and spent time trying to find out why.

For instance, a friend of mine Bob Hall – he's from Canada – **loves systematically dissecting high level movement patterns**. And not just baseball, but other sports as well.

Why?

Because of a rare illness his father had when Bob was a young boy, and also finding himself in a bad vehicle accident where he busted his neck up pretty bad, and afterward suffered splitting migraines for two years straight, day and night.

These two incidences drove him into medical journals and thick jargon Kinesiology textbooks. He played baseball and hockey in Canada back in his youth, but didn't end up in the professional ranks. If you talk to Bob – without knowing his educational background – you'd swear he has a PhD in human movement!

Now, **you don't need this much knowledge on the subject of coaching…just the right material**. Remember material beats method.

As an example, and we'll get into this more a bit later, but focusing a young team's efforts on playing catch. I heard 90% of batted balls in Little League game should be an out at first base. The reality is they're not, and as a coach, it's critical we focus our teams efforts on playing catch.

Virtue #2: Playing detective

This is like meeting someone on a blind date. To find out more about them, you have to play detective – by asking questions – to see if the mysterious person is a good fit for you.

In addition, we **coaches have to gain access to a player's learning processes**. Coaches have to really ask themselves, "Who are you really out here for?" Are we truly using empathy to understand where they're coming from or pushing our own agenda?

Great coaching is about getting information and figuring the pupil out. John Wooden once said,

> *"I am not going to treat you players all the same."*

We need different approaches for the learning styles of different athletes. I'll give you a fool-proof way to find out an athletes learning style in only 5-minutes much later in this book.

But for now, it's good to know,

Coaches need to have the curiosity of an investigative reporter…

> *"We have to always be checking in on them, because we need to know when they don't know."*

I love that statement, which came from Football Coach Tom Martinez in the book *The Talent Code*.

Virtue #3: Communication

When instructing your players, NEVER begin sentences with "Do you think…", "Please would you…", or "What about…?".

A great coach – like John Wooden – phrases instructions like a command, for example, "Now do X". Much like a GPS device, turn right, go straight, make a left.

Great coaches have to constantly change input…if A doesn't work, then try B…if not B, then try C.

Sometimes I spend eighty-percent of a session struggling with finding the right coaching cue, mental image, or metaphor…trying different ones, then one sticks. This is the one I send them home with to practice.

I'm continually checking in with my kids to make sure they understand. I learn more from them, than they probably learn from me!

Once the desired spot is achieved, then **move them to a** new more challenging spot. This ensures growth of mastering a particular skill.

Virtue #4: Theatrical honesty

Truly great teachers connect with students because of who they are, as in their moral standards. Your players need to know your playing background. Why you failed as a player, and maybe as a coach in the past. And what you're doing now that will make them better ball players.

I tell all my hitters and parents the reasons why I didn't play pro ball.

For example, one of my High School seniors was confronted by his coach about a certain hitting technique we were working on at the time. When asked who he was working with, he answered Joey Myers.

The coach knew me, and said,

"Well, I know Joey Myers didn't hit like that at Fresno State."

And my hitter didn't have a comeback for that. When he told me about the confrontation, I told him next time to say,

"Working hard got Joey Myers to college, but his hitting technique, at the time, was one major reason why he didn't push through his ceiling."

What's more…

'Do as I say, not as I do' is a load of horse crud. If you can't physically demonstrate what you want them to do, then you shouldn't be teaching it. If you remember, **John Wooden's Laws of learning were**: explanation, demonstration, imitation, correction, and repetition.

If you also recall, Wooden showed how to do the skill right, then how the athlete did it wrong, and then how to do it right again.

Now, I don't want to confuse you here…the point is that a coach must be able to demo a specific skill in order to teach it. This is what Wooden did quite often. Of course he couldn't dunk or run a 4.4 forty-yard dash…the point is that he can show his athletes how to do a pick and roll…demo the mechanics of a jump shot (although maybe not make it)…or be able to show how to rebound properly.

Just like in hitting, a coach should be able to demo what he's trying to get his hitter to do…maybe not hit a homerun (outcome based), but no matter how old or what gender a coach is, they should be able to demo forward momentum, or grip, or even spinal engine mechanics.

The best coaches are the ones who try out new hitting, fielding, or pitching concepts themselves BEFORE they teach it.

And lastly,

It would benefit every coach to better their communication skills. How do you do this? I've been a part of a local Toastmasters group for over 5-years now, and I think every coach should join a local club. What is Toastmasters? It's learning public speaking, leadership, and evaluation skills on a weekly or bi-monthly basis. For what you get, the bi-yearly fees are super cheap…at the time of this writing, renewing members pay $51 two times per year to participate in our club. You'll learn how-to:

- Influence your squad (in a good way),

- **Use storytelling to gain and keep interest**,
- Be able to simplify what you're trying to say and make it stick, and
- Improve your overall speaking ability – use of body language, tonal variety, how to craft your thoughts succinctly and quickly, remove crutch words like ah's and um's from your speech, and so on.

Our brain learns best by firing the circuit, getting feedback, and firing it again and again. That's what you do at Toastmasters to better your public speaking and communication skills.

Where do you find out about Toastmasters?

Just Google "toastmasters club [city and state you live in]"…so for me, I'd do a Google search like this: "toastmasters club fresno, ca". And Toastmasters is international, so if you're reading this in a country that isn't the USA, then add your country to the Google search terms.

I HIGHLY recommend joining Toastmasters to all coaches and teachers.

Remember, in this section, we analyzed the following Great Coaching ingredients:

1. Knowledge,
2. Playing detective,
3. Communication, and
4. Theatrical honesty.

Here are tools for your toolbox, on how-to communicate effectively with your players…

12

SECTION 1, CHAPTER 12

KNOWLEDGE: Motivating The Elephant

FOUR Fool-Proof Ways to Unlock an Athlete's Communication Style

From the International Youth Conditioning Association (IYCA), I wanted to share with you four categories of player ability and temperament. These are keys to igniting player motivation:

1. Low motivation-low skill,
2. Low motivation-high skill,
3. High motivation-low skill, and
4. High motivation-high skill.

Learning these guidelines **will allow you to understand and communicate more effectively** with each of your players, or setting them up in similar learning groups.

Low motivation-low skill – DIRECT

This type of player probably never played the sport before, or not very long. How do you appeal to this type of player? By being direct with your instruction, and having a purposeful direction for them. If you come across this type of athlete on your team at about the 10-12+ year old mark, then **a good solution would be to** refer them out to a trusted private instructor to "catch them up to speed".

Low motivation-high skill – INSPIRE

These players may find themselves at the top of your lineup, but may be a part of the hyper-parenting trap. They may be out there to please mom or dad. These players **need to be put on a pure praise-for-effort diet** ("you put a lot of hard work into that", "great work").

Whereas before they may have been getting praise-for-effort's evil twin: praise-for-intellect ("you're so smart" or "you're so talented").

Praise for effort will make all the difference. John Medina said one study showed how a scientist once got a chicken to turn the pages of a book – like he was reading it – by using continuous praise-for-effort. True story!

Actively inspire and encourage them.

High motivation-low skill – GUIDE

This is the "Rudy" of the team. You remember the movie *Rudy* right? If not, then rent and watch it on Netflix. There usually aren't too many of these, but when you have one, consider yourself lucky because they can inspire YOU and a whole team.

Another movie you can watch to further drill the idea is *Radio* with Cuba Gooding Jr.

One year when we played Stanford they had an honorary-player resembling the character Warren from the movie *Something About Mary*. He wore headphones everywhere he went during batting practice. At times, we had to protect him from batted balls when he was on our side. I thought this "player's" inclusion said A LOT about Stanford's program.

I'm not saying seek out kids with Developmentally Delayed Syndrome for your team, the preceding were just examples. You know what I mean.

Use guidance and goal setting with your *Rudys*. Get them to improve their skills through baby steps and tracking.

High motivation-high skill – DELEGATE

These are fun players to watch. And you won't have many of them, they're kind of an anomaly. They're ones you don't have to worry about on the field. With these players you want to make them a part of the decision making process. Practice drills, lineup creations, etc. Assign them to be the bridge between players and coaches. Seriously listen and consider their feedback.

They may be the Team Captains, the highest honor of any team. Think of Derek Jeter from the Yankees and Dustin Pedroia of the Red Sox. **These players are held to a higher standard, and represent the team on and off the field**. But make sure they make good decisions both on and off the field. They MUST be a role model.

Some are leaders-by-example, and some are more 'rah-rah' in nature. I was a leader by example. I didn't like being a cheerleader in front of the whole team all the time, and there's nothing wrong with that. Every player will be wired differently.

I hope these four fool-proof ways help unlock your Athletes' communication styles:

1. Low motivation-low skill,
2. Low motivation-high skill,
3. High motivation-low skill, and
4. High motivation-high skill.

Now for the backbone of speech syntax you'll be using throughout all your coaching – and parenting – days. **I guarantee you will after reading the science** backing the next section…

13

SECTION 1, CHAPTER 13

KNOWLEDGE: Motivating The Elephant

The Science of Praising-For-Effort

In this section, we'll be looking at:

- The "Praise-for" scientific study,
- Con's for Praise-for-intellect, and
- Five Reasons to Stop Saying "Good Job!"

This section is the heart and soul of *The Science of Sticky Coaching* book. It takes loads of cerebral energy to change the syntax of what you're saying and how you're saying it. The basic premise is **to stop celebrating generalized outcomes – or results – and promote the work that got the result**. The process over the outcomes, if you will.

In John Medina's book *Brain Rules for Baby*, he says:

> *"What separates high performers from low performers is not some divine spark. It is, the most recent findings suggest, a much more boring — but ultimately more controllable — factor. **All other things being equal, it is EFFORT**. The ability to focus one's attention, and then sustain that focus. Effort also involves impulse control and a persistent ability to delay gratification."*

Now, if you read David Epstein's book, *The Sports Gene: Inside the Science of Extraordinary Athletic Performance*, then you'll see Epstein come to the conclusion that it's both nature and nurture, not either or, that make extraordinary athletes. You can make your own decision.

The "Praise-for" scientific study

In *The Talent Code* by Daniel Coyle, he talked about Dr. Carol Dweck, a social psychologist at Stanford, who's been studying motivation for thirty years. She says,

"Left to our own devices, we go along in a pretty stable mindset," she said. *"But when we get a clear cue, a message that sends a spark, then boing, we respond."*

The following experiment **tested what changing the arrangement of six words could do to a child's psychological performance**...

Dr. Dweck did an experiment with 400 New York fifth graders. Kids were given a test of fairly easy puzzles, and afterwards were given a different mix of six-words.

She praised Group A with intelligence, *"You must be smart at this!"*

And she praised Group B for effort, *"You must have worked really hard."*

The Kids were tested a second time and were given the choice of a hard or easy test. Group A (praise-for-intellect) chose the easy test, while Group B (praise-for-effort) chose the hard test. Dweck explained,

"When we praise children for their intelligence, we tell them that's the name of the game: look smart, don't risk making mistakes."

The findings?

Quoted from *The Talent Code*,

"The praise-for-effort group improved their initial score by 30%, while the praised-for-intelligence group's score declined by 20%. All because of six short words."

Daniel Coyle said that true to the Dweck study, in each of the athletic hotbeds he visited from around the world, affirmed the value of effort and slow progress rather than innate talent or intelligence.

Praise needs to be earned. In which case, **we're affirming the struggle**. Dweck notes that,

"Motivation does not increase with increased levels of praise but often dips."

Motivational language often used refers to hopes, dreams, and affirmations ("Good job!" or "You're the best!" or "You're so talented!"). These statements are generalized, and therefore meaningless to performance.

Con's for Praise-for-intellect

The following ideas came from John Medina's *Brain Rules for Baby*...

What happens psychologically when you say *"You're so smart!"*?

*"First, your **child begins to perceive mistakes as failures**. Because you told her that success was due to some static ability over which she had no control, she starts to think of failure (such as a bad grade) as a static thing, too — now perceived as a lack of ability. Successes are thought of as gifts rather than the governable product of effort.*

*Second, perhaps as a reaction to the first, she **becomes more concerned with looking smart** than with actually learning something.*

*Third, she becomes **less willing to confront the reasons behind any deficiencies**, less willing to make an effort. Such kids have a difficult time admitting errors. There is simply too much at stake for the future.*

What should you say?

*'I'm so proud of you. You must have really studied hard.' This appeals to the controllable effort rather than to unchangeable talent. It's called **'growth mindset' praise**."*

Not to beat a dead horse here, but here's another article a good friend of mine – who has a Master's Degree in Child Development – sent me...

Five Reasons to Stop Saying "Good Job!" (http://bit.ly/stopsayinggoodjob)

Alfie Kohn authored and published this article in *Young Children's* magazine (2001). An abridged version of this article was published in *Parents* magazine in May 2000 with the title "Hooked on Praise." For a more detailed look at the issues discussed here — as well as a comprehensive list of citations to relevant research — please see the books *Punished by Rewards* and *Unconditional Parenting* by Alfie Kohn.

REASON #1: Manipulating Children

In the article, Rheta DeVries, a professor of education at the University of Northern Iowa, talks about how saying "Good job!" can be referred to as "sugar-coated control." This can look like tangible rewards – or even punishments because children are hungry for our approval.

It's a way of doing something for our children to comply with our wishes. As opposed to working with our children, such as asking them about how can what we've done affect other people...?

And in the words of Kohn:

> *"We have a responsibility not to exploit that dependence for our own convenience. A 'Good job!' to reinforce something that makes our lives a little easier can be an example of taking advantage of children's dependence. Kids may also come to feel manipulated by this, even if they can't quite explain why."*

REASON #2: Creating Praise Junkies

We may praise kids with a 'Good job!' because we really want to bolster their self esteem, but studies show the opposite actually happens. Praise like this can often make kids dependent on our feedback. Consider this study from the article:

> *"Mary Budd Rowe, a researcher at the University of Florida, discovered that students who were praised lavishly by their teachers were more tentative in their responses, more apt to answer in a questioning tone of voice ("Um, seven?").* **They tended to back off from an idea they had proposed as soon as an adult disagreed with them.** *And they were less likely to persist with difficult tasks or share their ideas with other students."*

In other words, praise makes a child feel more insecure than secure with themselves.

REASON #3: Stealing a Child's Pleasure

A child has the right to take pride in what they've learned how to do or done better than the last time. An adult telling them 'Good job!' is deciding – for the child – what to feel and when to feel it.

This is a form of positive judgment, just like 'Bad job!' would be a form of negative judgment. And just **like adults, kids don't like to be judged**.

In the words of Kohn:

> *"I cherish the occasions when my daughter manages to do something for the first time, or does something better than she's ever done it before. But I try to resist the knee-jerk tendency to say, "Good job!" because I don't want to dilute her joy. I want her to share her pleasure with me, not look to me for a verdict. I want her to exclaim, 'I did it!' (which she often does) instead of asking me uncertainly, 'Was that good?'"*

REASON #4: Losing Interest

"Good job!" may get children to keep doing what they did to get the praise, but early childhood education expert Lilian Katz warns, **"Once attention is withdrawn, many kids won't touch the activity again."** Now the point isn't to draw, to read, to think, to create – the point is to get the goody, whether it's an ice cream, a sticker, or a "Good job!"

In a study by Joan Grusec at the University of Toronto, young children who were frequently praised for displays of generosity tended to be slightly *less* generous on an everyday basis than other children were. Generosity became a means to an end.

Does praise motivate kids? Sure. **It motivates kids to get praise**.

REASON #5: Reducing Achievement

As Kohn says:

> *"Researchers keep finding that kids who are praised for doing well at a creative task tend to stumble at the next task – and they don't do as well as children who weren't praised to begin with.*
>
> *Why does this happen? Partly because the praise creates pressure to "keep up the good work" that gets in the way of doing so. Partly because their interest in what they're doing may have declined. Partly because they become less likely to take risks – a prerequisite for creativity – once they start thinking about how to keep those positive comments coming."*

World renown personal and business development coach Anthony Robbins talks about the power of word syntax. Changing words around can make a big difference. For instance, "The dog bit Johnny," versus "Johnny bit the dog." Especially for Johnny!

Changing the way you praise young athletes can make them work harder for you. AND, they also get the benefit of not feeling manipulated, getting their independence, pleasure, interest, and sense of achievement taken away.

A good friend of mine Kari Bowers has a Masters in Child Development, and shared with me a PDF she developed for her parents on **changing word syntax to more positively communicate with their children**.

Again, this applies to how coaches talk with their players.

CLICK the following link for the "USING LANGUAGE PDF":

http://gohpl.com/praise4effortpdf

For instance, saying 'You did it!" or "There you go..." instead of "Good job!". The above PDF really goes into different situations and details, so I highly suggest you study it and change your syntax!

Remember, in this section, we looked at:

- The "Praise-for" scientific study,
- Con's for Praise-for-intellect, and
- Five Reasons to Stop Saying "Good Job!"

14

SECTION 1, CHAPTER 14

KNOWLEDGE: Motivating The Elephant

THREE Unique Ways to Ignite Motivation

In this section, we're going over:

- How to Keep It Simple Sally (KISS),
- How a nice, easy, and pleasant environment shuts effort OFF, and
- The Andrew Jones Effect.

Most of the time for my parents (and myself), motivation (and inspiration) is a challenge. What is it that gets the elephant moving? Let's find out…

How-to Keep It Simple Sally (KISS)

As Tim Ferris says in the meta-learning portion of his NY Times Bestselling book *The Four Hour Chef*:

> *"And so we learn a lesson: it's the burden on working memory that makes something easy or hard. Overloading our circuits with variable pacing, performing multiple new skills ambidextrously and simultaneously, and much more. It's an interference hail storm."*

Keep things simple. Leo Babauta in his blog ZenHabits.net, puts mastering a new skill or stopping a bad habit into perspective:

- If you focus on ONE thing at a time? You'll have an 85% success rate.
- Two focuses at a time? Your success-rate DROPS to 35%.
- Three or more focuses at a time? Dips below a 10% success rate.

After working with any one of my hitting students, **I try and ONLY prescribe one hitting drill for them to master per week**. Any more than that, and I'm setting them up to fail.

Every coach makes the mistake of over-coaching. I've done it! With younger athletes, if the issue with the team is playing catch, then why are we working on hitting? Remember, good pitching and defense beats a good hitting team.

Just like when you have multiple browsers open on your computer, your computer crashes, freezes, or slows down. So does the human brain. **We're not very efficient multi-taskers, especially between the ages of seven to thirteen years old.**

Nothing motivates an elephant more than a one focused task.

The other thing I do is tell my hitters to give me four to five days per week to do their hitting homework, and only 5-minutes per day. WHY only five minutes? Because it holds the elephant's motivation.

How a nice, easy, and pleasant environment shuts effort OFF

I shared with you earlier how John Medina in his bestselling book *Brain Rules for Baby*, said that the **brain learns to survive, and doesn't survive to learn. As long as we feel safe, we're free to learn.** Overwhelming research proves this.

However, just like 'Good job!' can shut down effort for youth athletes, so can variables such as:

- Hip newly designed uniforms every year,
- Playing on the best manicured fields,
- Hitting with the latest-and-greatest bats every year (it's not the arrow, it's the Indian by the way),
- Fielding with new professional leather every season, and
- Always throwing bullpens with 'pretty' baseballs.

According to Daniel Coyle's research in *The Talent Code*,

> "John Bargh a psychologist at Yale University pioneered automaticity* studies in the mid-1980's, said "If we're in a nice, easy, pleasant environment, we naturally shut off effort...why work? But if people get the signal that it's rough, they get motivated now. A nice, well-kept tennis academy gives them the luxury future right now — of course they'd be de-motivated. They can't help it."

(*From Wikipedia, Automaticity means: the ability to do things without occupying the mind with the low-level details required, allowing it to become an automatic response pattern or habit. It is usually the result of learning, repetition, and practice.)

You remember Rocky, in the movie Rocky III, going back to train at Appollo Creed's old stomping grounds when he had to fight Clubber Lang (Mr. T) right? The old hole in the wall?!

During my first three years of Fresno State, we used uniforms whose design was over thirty years old. We didn't have new baseballs to practice with everyday. **We used our baseballs until the cover was tearing off of them**...and this was at the Division 1 college level!

We had three levels of used baseballs. The new ones went to the pitchers' bullpens, games, and batting practice on game days. The gently used ones would be utilized in team drills, and the heavily used baseballs would be banished to our hitting stations.

Here's another example of a not-so-pleasant environment,

Why do you think Caribbean, Venezuelan, Puerto Rican, Cuban, and Dominican players seem to be hungry to make it to 'The Show'? Joe DiMaggio once said,

> "A ball player has to be kept hungry to become a big leaguer. That's why no boy from a rich family has ever made the big leagues."

Sure this is a common generalization, because surely Ken Griffey Jr., Barry Bonds, and the Cal Ripken brothers weren't for want growing up. And The Great Depression was just getting underway when Joe said this.

But, I bet if you looked at the background of every Big Leaguer ever, you'd get a sense that for quite a few, a low socio-economic status was a huge driver in igniting their motivation to play in the Big Leagues. The point is motivation here. Is it impossible to make it to the Bigs coming from a rich family? No. Do athletes who grow up in a low socio-economic environment have more motivation to get out of it? For some, yes! It takes A LOT of motivation to stick with the dream of making it to "The Show." And every little bit counts. But it doesn't mean parents well endowed with earnings don't have a chance. There are many things you'll learn throughout this book that will ignite motivation, so stick with me here.

The Andrew Jones Effect

In Daniel Coyle's book *The Talent Code*, he says:

> *"Having a model who is just like you, who's "made it", to motivate. In school, it can be the goal for college to drive motivation. Bring these goal cues up constantly.* **Make them feel like it's going to happen, but first they must get 'this' right..."**

Coyle uses the example of Curacao youth baseball. They've become a hot-spot for Major League recruiters as of late. Their Little Leaguers are consistently competing at the youth World Series level every year, and it all started because of a player named Andrew Jones. Curacao was his homeland.

The Andrew Jones Effect is because he became an instant role model the minute he 'made it', to all those aspiring young Curacao baseball players.

Even if you don't have a local MLB'er to be the igniting role model, in Curacao, their fields are set up so that Little Leaguers can see the older players on the big fields. This **gives the younger players easy access to watch and mimic their favorite players**. It's a revolving door of motivation and inspiration.

Having your hitter become a student of the game works too. I used to read auto/biographies on Ted Williams, Babe Ruth, Joe DiMaggio, "Shoeless" Joe Jackson, and Tom Seaver. Going to and watching pro baseball and softball games helps as well. Our athletes should be encouraged to do these things and not forced.

Remember, in this section, we went over:

- Keeping it simple with one focus,
- How a nice, easy, and pleasant environment shuts effort OFF, and
- The Andrew Jones Effect: having someone – a role model – to strive for. To becomes a student of the game.

15

SECTION 1, CHAPTER 15

KNOWLEDGE: Motivating The Elephant

THREE Commandments to Coaching a Moral Athlete

Here, we're going to talk about:

- Setting up clear consistent rules and rewards,
- Swift punishment, and
- Rules that are explained.

As John Medina states in his bestselling book *Brain Rules for Baby*,

> *"On rules and discipline: the evolutionary need for safety is so powerful,* **the presence of rules themselves often communicates safety to children."**

Setting up clear consistent rules and rewards

Rules need to be reasonable and clear. As a coach, have a 'ten commandments' list that's typed, laminated, and pinned up on the fence for all to see. My high school and college coaches always assigned field duties to us for field and equipment maintenance.

Coach Batesole at Fresno State **had a sticker reward system** – much like The Ohio State Buckeyes do – we could earn a sticker for our helmet by knocking in a two-out RBI, crushing a double to score the go-ahead run in the late innings, or hitting a bases loaded double. The stickers can really ignite players because each one wants to have the most stickers to show off. It just sucks having to take the stickers off each season.

Above-all,

You must be warm and accepting while administering your set rules. **If you're angry and/or judgmental, then the survival instinct sets in and the child shuts down learning,** and is more likely to become defiant.

You can also offer praise when a rule is followed, and also in the absence of bad behavior (see *The Science of Praising-for-Effort section*).

Another good tip would be to video yourself coaching to analyze later. This can give you instant feedback to tinker and improve upon. This is something John Wooden would do in this day and age.

Swift punishment

Whatever your rules say, the punishment needs to quickly follow a breech. For instance, physical mistakes can be forgiven, but not mental mistakes...pitchers not knowing where to throw in a double play situation...fielders not communicating with each other and or throwing to the wrong base...**base-running mistakes also show a lapse in judgment**.

Just like punishing a dog for pooping on the carpet three hours later is ineffective, so is the case with young athletes. Strike when the iron is hot, and the poop is fresh. And remember, be warm and accepting when administering your rules.

Rules that are explained

Here's an example WITHOUT using an explanation:

"Don't touch the dog, or you'll get a time-out."

Now here it is WITH explanation:

"Don't touch the dog, or you'll get a time-out. The dog has a bad temper, and I don't want you to get bitten."

You'll also find this is the common denominator in *The Science of Praise-for-Effort* section in this Course. Instead of spouting broad generalized statements of what not to do...add the rationale backing it.

When we have clear and reasonable rules, they're administered in a warm and accepting way, then explaining the rationale won't be that difficult.

I learned to appreciate – the hard way – this way of coaching a moral athlete with Coach Bennett. **Everything about his coaching style was consistent and predictable, all the way down to the rules, and their enforcement**. And when a rule was breeched, we were given the rationale behind it.

When a player doesn't know what to expect from a coach, it could make practices and games really unpredictable and not fun. I tell all my players, this game is built on consistency. **When the brain doesn't know what to expect, it will be difficult to get consistent performance out of the player.**

Remember, when it comes to the three commandments to coaching a moral athlete, we talked about:

- Setting clear consistent rules and rewards,
- Swift punishment, and
- Rules that are explained.

16

SECTION 1, CHAPTER 16

KNOWLEDGE: Shaping The Path

THREE Unique Top Level Coaching Secrets

This is where we'll begin to introduce coaching techniques to help 'feel' the path to skill mastery. We'll be going over:

- Using Switch-words,
- Backward Chaining: training the 'negative', and
- Chunking (whole-part-whole) teaching.

I use all – if not a combination – of these coaching techniques when teaching my students how-to hit.

Using Switch-Words

According to the International Youth Conditioning Association (IYCA), switch-words are...

> *"Simple one-word declarations that are thought to enable the subconscious mind to trigger a particular behavior pattern or thought process. Many coaches tend to employ long and unfocused verbal commands to encourage action or behavior in young athletes."*

For example, if a coach wants a player to run faster, they may say,

> *"Get there! Come on! Let's go!"*

But the problem with these cues is they're unfocused, inconsistent, and doesn't give the brain a solid message of what to do to get faster.

Another example would be a coach wanting a player to jump higher, so he yells,

> *"Get off the ground! Get up there!"*

Again, unfocused, inconsistent, and it sends an unclear message to the brain.

Here's a list of desired actions, and their Switch-words developed from the best in IYCA coaches:

- Skipping or expressing rhythm = FLOW
- Producing force = THROUGH or DRIVE
- Speed of reaction = FIRE
- Running faster = HIT
- Gaining range of motion = BIG
- Increasing torso strength = BRACE or SET

When it comes to hitting...

Typically, I start with a sentence string of words, and then whittle it down to one switch-word when I'm working on a new skill with a student. I always thought I was being lazy doing this, but there are actually scientific studies backing how effective Switch-words can be to instruction.

Backward Chaining: training the 'negative'

In high school, my teammates would get a kick out of my best friend doing Hideo Nomo's pitching delivery in reverse. It was a riot!

According to the IYCA, Backward Chaining involves...

> *"Teaching a skill set in reverse sequence, thereby affording more opportunity for practice of the components of the skill that occur later in the movement. Most recently, the approach has gained increased notoriety in baseball training circles, where Wolforth (2001), utilizing what he refers to as "back shaping," has claimed tremendous gains in pitching velocity and a dramatically reduced rate of injury in baseball athletes."*

Tim Ferris in his book, *The Four Hour Chef* (4HC), even calls this "upside down" training. He said, when learning the Tango in a short amount of time that learning the female role helped a lot.

How can coaches do this with their players? Either:

1. **Practicing the skill in reverse** (like my buddy did with Hideo Nomo's windup), or
2. Executing the skill on the opposite side, for instance a natural righty hitting left handed.

On number two above, a guy I met who competed at the college level in Shot Put told me that a well-known Olympic Shot Putter said something like,

> *"You can only throw as far as your weak side allows you to."*

This is also a way to balance the body out. A balanced body is a high performance body. But that's a talk for another day. The point is, **coaches can really get insight from having their players practice backward-chaining on their unnatural side.**

I mentioned my friend Thomari who founded a local traveling baseball organization called Team Avenue. Well, one day he was working with a high school sophomore on switch-hitting in the batting cage next to me. I could immediately tell a difference in tempo from the hitter's natural and unnatural sides.

After his round, Thomari asked for my input. I told the player go back to hitting from his natural right-side, but swing with the same tempo as he did with his unnatural left-side.

The results were shocking!

He instantly began hitting the ball better up the middle and to the opposite field whereas everything before was going down the left field line. He was pulling everything before and over-rotating. Yes, hitters can over-rotate.

Backward-chaining works, no joke. We don't have to make everyone into a switch-hitter or thrower. However, by making players repeat mechanics on their opposite side, it forces their brain to think!

Daniel Coyle calls this Deeper Practice, and it's what babies do…**baby steps are the royal road to skill mastery**.

Chunking (whole-part-whole) teaching

This is the best teaching method I've found in baseball and softball. Here's what the IYCA says about the whole-part-whole teaching method:

> *"Practically speaking, young athletes of today who are oftentimes highly dependent upon visual learning stimuli may benefit from **seeing a given skill expressed in its entirety before working on the steps necessary for successful performance**. For example, a young athlete attempting to perfect a basketball jump shot might prefer to see and attempt the skill in its entirety before attempting to master the finer aspects of performance then training the total skill again."*

Typically the whole-part-whole method is used to learn more complex skills. I use this and the progression-part-whole method as well, which is breaking – say the skill of hitting – down into parts. **Once a part is mastered, then we layer it with the next level. It's like building a cake**.

For instance, for fielding and throwing, you may teach the players a proper static (feet cemented in the ground) fielding position where they pair up and roll each other groundballs. Once they master the routine groundball position, then you layer back & fore-hand groundballs…then you layer footwork to the different groundballs…then you layer playing catch…then random groundballs and throws to first. And so on, making it one-step harder.

But a lot of the times, my students want to see me to show them the whole swing first, then go into the breakdown (whole-part-whole). **It's not showing off, but if you're going to teach it, you should be able to demonstrate it**. Remember, 'demonstrate' was part of John Wooden's ten coaching commandments, so if you can't show it, get someone who can.

We went over three different ideas that appeal to shaping the path:

- Using Switch-words,
- Backward Chaining: training the 'negative', and
- Chunking (whole-part-whole) teaching.

——

This concludes the portion of the book labeled KNOWLEDGE. Remember, at the start we were **looking to equip inexperienced coaches, parents, and organizational leaders on how-to effectively run their teams**. This section was about teaching and doing things right. In other words, coaching "effectiveness".

I even shared the HPL Coaches Credo that I recommended taking a screen shot of and/or printing out. The rest of the KNOWLEDGE portion of the book was about the art of sticky coaching, where we applied – and will continue to apply – the following metaphor:

- Guiding the rider (planning and organization),
- Moving the elephant (emotions), and
- Shaping the path (doing things right).

Now, it's off to see what science says about **how athletes learn**…

17

SECTION 2, CHAPTER 1

LEARNING

How This Section Will Work...

In this section, we'll be looking at how 'they' learn. In other words, optimizing how young athletes acquire new skills, and maintain a rich soil for learning.

In a survey, I asked my subscribers what the two most frustrating things were about coaching Little League. Now, here **are common frustrations coming from coaches** that were Learning-related:

- Athletes don't listen or retain instruction
- Parents don't practice with kids at home
- Athletes not wanting to be at practice (practice isn't fun and engaging)
- Practice swing v. game swing difference
- The right amount of reps?
- Practice length and frequency

Have you experienced or wondered about any of the points above? What does the science say?

As we dive into the following information, I'll do my best to address these common frustrations with what Science and the Top 1% of coaches say about them.

We'll keep close to the rider, elephant, and path metaphor as we dig into how-to make scientific coaching sticky...

18

SECTION 2, CHAPTER 2

LEARNING: Guiding The Rider

The Ancient Secret to Growing a Super-Athlete

In this section, we'll be discussing three things related to our biological need to adapt and survive. Here's what we'll be talking about:

- What is the purpose of myelin in the brain?
- "It's not how fast you can do it, but how slow you can do it correctly."
- Is struggling an option?

What is the purpose of myelin in the brain?

According to Daniel Coyle's research in *The Talent Code*...

Myelin is a protein in the brain that's responsible for reinforcing skill acquisition. I explain it to my athletes like this...

Imagine a piece of copper wire (a nerve fiber in the brain) being wrapped and insulated with duct tape (the myelin). Every move we make or thought we take, myelin (the duct tape) wraps thicker around the nerve fiber (the copper wire).

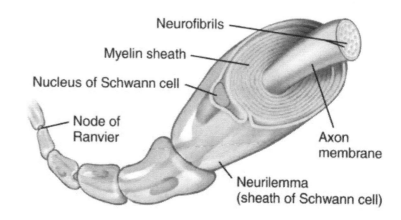

Anatomy of a myelin nerve fiber, photo courtesy: TheClickerCenterBlog.com

For a specific movement or thought pattern, **thicker wrapped duct tape (myelin) around a nerve fiber is like a high-speed internet connection** for an athlete when it comes to movement patterns – good or bad.

In other words, when an athlete starts learning a new skill – or part of a complex skill – their movements start out clunky and awkward. But the more they practice the skill, the smoother the motion, and more automatic the movement becomes.

The less like a robot they tend to move.

People often mistake this for 'muscle memory'. **Muscles are dumb, the brain delegates to them when needed.** It's the Central Nervous System (CNS) that we're keying in on here.

I tell my students that each movement we practice is a needle touching down on your favorite record. The more you play that record, the deeper the needle wears the groove, the deeper the groove, the more set-in the movement pattern.

This goes for bad motor patterns as well. Sometimes we have to spend A LOT of time in the beginning, unwinding bad habits. Paul Chek of the CHEK Institute says **it takes three-thousand repetitions to unwind a bad habit** and three hundred to set it straight.

What's great though, is the fact myelin (the duct tape) doesn't care how much money you make…where you live in the world…what color skin you have…or whether you're male or female, big or small.

Nope.

All myelin cares about is what you do! If you don't 'DO', then you don't thicken the duct tape around the copper wires in your brain.

Daniel Coyle warns about what kryptonite is to a high-level athlete…

Keeping them from practicing for a month! Their 'duct tape' will start to unravel, and they'll begin losing the efficiency (insulation) in their new learned skill.

As football coach Tom Martinez put it in *The Talent Code*…

"It's not how fast you can do it, but how slow you can do it correctly"

I use it all the time with my young hitters. Most times I see kids trying to swing as hard as they can. When we first start training, it's hard for them to sacrifice performance for development.

I tell them they NEED to slow the new movement down because **we have to allow the brain to catch up with the body**. As they start to wind the duct tape tighter and thicker around their copper wire, then we can progress closer to game tempo.

Here's how I use rep-tempo to teach new movement skills:

- **Beginner to movement skill** = 40% swing tempo until 85-90% accurate execution
- **Intermediate to movement skill** = 50-75% swing tempo until 85-90% accurate execution
- **Advanced to movement skill** = 85-90% swing tempo (*game-speed), but must be 85-90% accurate in the execution of the skill.

(*I consider eighty-five to ninety-percent swing tempo, game-speed. Anything higher than that and the players tend to start tensing up unwanted muscle (neck, upper trap, and shoulders), and slowing bat speed down. Read the following…)

It's eerie how the eighty-five to ninety-percent game-speed tempo shows up in a couple other common competitive human movements:

- **Cycling**: 85-90 revolutions per minute are what's optimum, whether going uphill or downhill – because remember, you're expected to adjust the gears as necessary.
- **Running long distance**: each time your right hand swings up should equal 85-90 times per minute, whether faster/slower running speed, uphill/downhill.

The point is, to progress a new skill properly, it's not how fast we can do it, but how slow we can do it right. I also say, "How fast you can possibly go, under complete control." Remember, we're looking for at least ninety-percent proficiency here, then progress the tempo. For hitting, this also goes for progressing dry reps, tee, soft toss, and LIVE reps.

Is struggling an option?

According to Daniel Coyle and his research, struggling with learning a new skill ISN'T an option. It's a biological requirement. In the book, Coyle talks about – through his research – the best way to fire a circuit:

1. **Fire it**,
2. **Attend to mistakes**,
3. **Then fire it again**.

…wash, rinse, and repeat.

Sorry there's no magical formula for creating repeatable 'muscle memory'. No pill you can just take. It's primal actually. It requires NO internet, video gaming, or the best in sporting equipment. Just follow the THREE SIMPLE RULES above.

Here's a good example of "the struggle" everyone should understand…

Have you ever been told someone's name and five seconds later forgot it? **Studies show that if you try and come up with it yourself** (firing the circuit), you'll more likely remember it later, especially if you say it wrong (attending to mistakes), then fire it again.

BUT, if instead you ask for it again without coming up with it on your own, then chances are you'll forget it.

As parents and coaches, it's difficult to see our kids and players struggle and fail with something new. But it's essential to their growth and development. Daniel Coyle reveals the deep dark secret of the struggle:

> *"It's about working on technique, seeking constant feedback, and focusing ruthlessly on shoring up weaknesses."*

What's funny is babies aren't taught how to roll, crawl, or walk. They work on their technique while gravity gives them constant feedback (they fall or they don't fall), and then focus ruthlessly on shoring up their weaknesses.

Coyle says:

*"Staggering babies embody the deepest truth about deep practice: to get good, it's helpful to be willing, or even enthusiastic, about being bad. **Baby steps are the royal road to skill.**"*

I often ask my students if they want their struggle to be longer or shorter. They always say shorter.

However, time tells me whether they truly believe that or not. I can always tell if they've been practicing, so I tell them not to just feed me what I want to hear. If they want to decrease their struggle time, then they have to 'DO'.

To struggle isn't an option. It's a biological requirement.

Remember, in this section, we analyzed three ancient secrets to growing a super athlete:

- What is the purpose of myelin in the brain?
- "It's not how fast you can do it, but how slow you can do it correctly." And,
- Is struggling an option?

This was my 9-mo-old son Noah learning to walk, "enthusiastically being bad"

19

SECTION 2, CHAPTER 3

LEARNING: Guiding The Rider

How-To Develop Youth Athletic Motor Skills in FOUR Easy Stages...

In this section, we're going to talk about what the International Youth Conditioning Association (IYCA) calls the four stages of athletic motor skill development:

1. **Movement Foundation** (2-5 yo),
2. **Guided Discovery** (6-9 yo),
3. **Learning Exploration** (10-13 yo), and
4. **Train with Application (14+).**

You see, every child develops movement skill through a sequence of stages or periods that are age-related, but not necessarily age-determined.

According to the IYCA, motor development status is determined by many factors, including but not limited to:

- **Environment** (parents, siblings, facilities, coaches, opportunities to develop),
- **Socio-cultural** (socioeconomic status, cultural beliefs, gender stereotypes),
- **Individual** (age, cognitive abilities, motivation, self-efficacy, self-worth, perceived competence, gender).

Let's begin talking about...

Movement Foundation (2-5 yo)

This period is basic locomotion such as: running, jumping, hopping, and leaping. Also object manipulation such as: throwing, catching, striking, and kicking.

This is where we want to **start putting emphasis on praising effort** rather than on intellect or generalized outcomes. We want to also be using positive encouragement and feedback (See *The Science of Praising-For-Effort* section earlier in the book).

Above all, we coaches need to emphasize that effort equals success. Twenty-to-thirty-minute sessions are plenty during this period.

Guided Discovery (6-9 yo)

In this period, we want to continue promoting that effort equals success. We also want to pay close attention to body type here. This age of athlete will start to vary in height, weight, and muscle development.

This is a great time to **transition basic locomotion into various sport skills**, games like hopping like a frog, crawling like a bear, and cleaning out the backyard.

A dynamic warm-up can be introduced along with functional strength body weight movements such as lunging, squatting, pushing, pulling, bending, twisting, and single leg stepping patterns. DO NOT promote these movements as "work" or "punishment" yet.

Learning Exploration (10-13 yo)

Be sensitive to others' developmental background here. For instance, females demonstrate lower fundamental movement skill than males in this age range.

Training backgrounds will vary, so study the *FOUR Fool-Proof Ways to Unlock an Athlete's Communication Style (Ability & Temperament)* in the KNOWLEDGE section of the book.

Be careful with an athlete's weight training schedule, and playing in multiple throwing related sports, which could lead to shoulder overuse. Sometimes I may get a hitter who's pitching and playing on two separate baseball travel teams, getting ready for football season as their team's quarterback, and doing a lot of over-head shoulder and bench press stuff in the weight room. **This spells D-I-S-A-S-T-E-R for the shoulder. Be sensitive to this as a coach.**

This is a great time to start using body-weight exercises for dynamic balance, mobilization/stabilization, and strength training. DO NOT strength train until they show perfect form in the functional movements mentioned in Guided Discovery FIRST!

Train with Application (14+)

DO NOT attempt to "catch-up" low developed athletes here. If you do, then you're asking for trouble with burnout, low self-esteem, and/or injury. Refer the athlete out to a competent private instructor to catch them up to the team's speed.

Youth physical development takes years to promote, and **progressing specific training levels cannot be "skipped"** in order to promote success in the short-term.

Remember, as a youth coach, you're in the business of player development, NOT winning. Let their High School Varsity, College, and Professional coaches worry about winning.

To recap, the International Youth Conditioning Association calls the four stages of athletic motor skill development:

1. Movement Foundation (2-5 yo),
2. Guided Discovery (6-9 yo),
3. Learning Exploration (10-13 yo), and
4. Train with Application (14+).

Youth athletes develop at different points, so **remember the above stages are age-related, and not necessarily age determined.**

20

SECTION 2, CHAPTER 4

LEARNING: Guiding The Rider

How-to Productively Transfer Practice to Game Reps

Here's what we're going to cover in this CHAPTER:

- **How to train "game-ready" hitters**
- How to find out a player's dominant learning style in 5-mins
- How to apply 'training-ugly' principles to practice
- Coaching feedback and practice time: **how much is too much, and when is it not enough?**

Let's get started…

How to Train "Game Ready" Hitters

Why do you think one of the most asked questions I get is, how to transition grooved batting practice swings into game-swing performance?

To answer this common coaching challenge, let me tell you a story…

There was a young Greek boy, named Milo of Croton, who was told by his parents to carry their baby bull into town, to get milk and feed him.

Milo carried this bull into town day after day, week after week, and month after month.

The bull kept getting bigger with each passing day, and as a result, Milo also grew bigger and stronger.

This young Milo ended up becoming one of the most revered wrestlers in Greek history.

According to Sports-Training-Advisor.com,

"The Principle of Specificity refers to the type of changes the body makes in response to sports training. Very simply, what you do is what you get."

Milo got bigger and stronger because the bull's weight progressively increased.

So, what does the Principle of Specificity have to do with transitioning a five-o-clock hitter into a game crusher?

EVERYTHING!

In baseball or softball, imagine a "shot clock" between pitches.

What do you estimate that shot clock would count to?

10-20 seconds between pitches?

In addition, a hitter will get, on average, three chances to swing the bat...three strikes. Sometimes more or sometimes less...but let's use THREE as an average.

This same hitter may get FOUR at-bats per game.

So, this hitter may get TWELVE opportunities to swing the bat in a game.

Also, most likely, there will be more than 10-20 seconds between swings.

The point is this; **hitters MUST make every swing count.**

In addition, and unlike golf, there are two major elements included in competing at the plate...pitch selection, and being on-time.

If we're looking at the principle of Specificity – or *what you do is what you get* – then **what would training look like to address the environment of game swings?**

I'll give you an example of something that DOES NOT help hitters adapt to the demands of a game at-bat...

Would a drill like rapid fire soft toss or rapid fire batting practice help hitters? Tossing or throwing a batting practice pitch every 2-4 seconds...

NO.

Before you get into the argument, *"Well, that drill is for developing quick hands"*.

If that's what you're thinking, then you're missing the forest for the trees.

The hands get quicker and more forceful when the swing is driven by the Spinal Engine. In other words, quick hands without effective Spinal Engine mechanics, is like swatting flies.

Think about the force of a boxer's jab versus his knockout punch.

If the pitcher had three baseballs to start, and the name of the game was how efficient she could release those three pitches in quick succession to the hitter, then rapid fire soft and LIVE toss would be the way to train.

But it's not.

So how do we train hitters in the cages to maximize every swing?

> 1. **Make sure the hitter understands they should be breathing heavier after 5 swings.**
> 2. Only have hitters take three to five swings per round, and then take a short coach's evaluation break (more on giving feedback to hitters shortly).
> 3. As coach, take your time replacing the ball on a tee, or serving up another soft or LIVE toss...give the hitter a chance to reset.

Look, hitting is a sprint, not a marathon. More effort, higher intensity, less reps. Just like you wouldn't do marathon training for a 100-meter sprint competition.

Hitting is not about taking 100 swings to get into a "groove" or "rhythm".

What do you think the swing intensity of a 50-pitch round batting practice looks like?

About 70% or less because the hitter would need to conserve energy to get through the long arse round!

What do you think practicing 70% swing intensity does to game timing, if in the game, the hitter is expected to use 100% swing intensity?

The hitter would have to start their swing much earlier in game at-bats to compensate for the variance in practice swings.

So why not practice 100% swing intensity in practice, so the hitter doesn't have to re-calibrate their timing in games?

The only time it's okay to turn down swing RPM's during practice is when working on something mechanically.

Before getting into "training ugly", I want to go over…

How to find out a Player's Dominant Learning Style in 5-mins

I mentioned a coach's evaluation between five-swing rounds…

It's during this time, coach will quiz the hitter to see how body aware they were with the swings they took.

It is in these questions, that you can learn a player's learning-style within minutes.

The VAK Model, as it is called, is according to the science of Neuro-Linguistic Programming, or NLP for short, which is what world-renown, public-speaker, Tony Robbins uses in his programs.

VAK stands for Visual, Auditory, and Kinesthetic (or feel).

A player's dominant learning style can be tipped off within minutes, by looking at where the hitter's eyes go immediately after being asked a question…

- **If the eyes go UP** and to the left or right, then they may be primarily a visual learner.
- **If the eyes go SIDE-TO-SIDE**, then they may be primarily an auditory learner. And,
- **If the eyes go DOWN** and to the left, right, or straight forward, then they may be primarily a kinesthetic (or feel) learner.

I say "may be primarily", because in 5 minutes, you're getting a ballpark estimate. Over time, with a particular hitter, you'll be more certain of their primary learning style.

You'll also notice their second "go-to" eye location, which is helpful if your primary learning style coaching cue doesn't seem to be working.

For instance, **if I notice a player's eyes consistently going down when answering my questions, and occasionally they go up…then I know that hitter has a primarily *feel* learning style with *visual* as secondary. So, I can play with those two.**

What are some coaching questions using the VAK model?

Visual cues:

- "Can you *see* what you just did there?"
- "*Look* at what you did on swing number-3…"
- "Was the difference between those swings *black and white*, or kind of *grey*?"

Auditory cues:

- "How did the *sound* of impact differ from swing one and swing four?"
- "Does the answer springy fascia *ring a bell*?"
- "Notice the *discord* at impact when you're off the sweet spot?"

Kinesthetic cues:

- "Can you *feel* the difference between the two swings?"
- "I want you to *hold* your swing position at landing…"
- "You hit that ball like a *ton of bricks*!"

Now, that you have this tool in your belt; let's move on to discussing...

How to Apply 'Training Ugly' Principles to Practice

I'm going to share with you a couple studies from Peter C. Brown's book, *Make It Stick*, to help illustrate this section...

Hitters of the Cal Poly baseball team were split up into two groups throughout the season.

Group one hitters are thrown the following pitches at practice:

- 15 fastballs,
- 15 curveballs, and
- 15 changeups.

Group two hitters are thrown a random mix of these three pitches at practice.

Which group do you think did better throughout the season?

The Massed Practice group one, also known as Blocked, Or the Random Practice group two?

Group one did better in the initial practice rounds, however group TWO did better throughout the season.

WHY?

A classroom of 4th graders were split up into two groups, A and B.

Group A practiced throwing bean bags into a bucket that was 3-feet away for 15 minutes.

Group B practiced throwing bean bags into two buckets, one was 2-feet away and the other was 4-feet away.

At the end of 15-minutes, both groups were tested throwing the bean bags in one 3-foot bucket...

Which group did better?

Group B did, who practiced throwing into the two buckets.

WHY?

Massed (or Blocked) Practice versus Random Practice

Why did the Cal Poly baseball study turn out like it did?

...and what about the bean bag study?

YouTuber Trevor Ragan gives this a name, 'Training Ugly'.

I like 'training goofy' because that's what if feels like, or using variance.

He says effectively learning a sport skill, requires three steps:

1. **Read**
2. **Plan**
3. **Do**

In the random-pitched group of Cal Poly baseball players, and the two-bucket distance bean bag group, the participants had to Read, Plan, and Do. The latter "Do" step is the execution of technique.

In the Massed or Block Practice groups, the "Read" and "Plan" steps were virtually removed from the motor-skill-acquisition-equation.

According to Random versus Block Practice studies in basketball, golf, and baseball, **this matters A LOT when transitioning and retaining sport skills into games because that's how the competitive environment is...seemingly random.**

And in those studies, skill retention rates went up in games over 40% more when Random Practice was instituted over Blocked.

For a young athlete, 'training ugly' or "goofy":

- Is more challenging,
- Will be more frustrating, and as a result, they'll make more mistakes,
- **Is better for them**, and
- Prepares them better for game situations.

We'll look at how to apply the 'Training Ugly' Principle to hitters in a moment, but first…

The Goldilocks Golden Rule

You've heard the story of *Goldilocks and the Three Bears,* right?

In the bears' kitchen, Goldilocks didn't want the porridge that was too hot or too cold, she wanted the one that was just right.

I talk to my hitters about mechanics this way.

Let me give you another example.

On the Hardcore History podcast, the host **shared how the Germans calibrated their big artillery fire at the trenches of the French and British during World War 1**.

The Allied Nations would be sitting in their 8-foot trench and hear a whistling overhead…and they'd watch a gigantic German artillery shell fly over their trenches, land and explode about one mile away.

Then, another whistling, but this time the gigantic German artillery shell would land about one mile in front of their open trench.

Guess where the next one landed…

Near their trench!! And from there on out, the British and French military forces were bombarded with reigning SUPER-heavy German artillery from overhead.

What were the Germans doing?

It has a name, according to Marine Colonel, Mark Coast, who's father to two of my hitters in San Diego, and who's a Primary Firearms and Tactical Instructor for Navy Seal and Marine snipers.

The Germans were doing what's called the 'Standard Artillery Round Adjustment Method'.

Again, coming back to the bean bag study and the Goldilocks Golden Rule.

So,

How to Apply 'Training Ugly' Principles to Practice?

The following, is what I use with my hitters on a daily basis, but is definitely not exhaustive of what you could come up with.

In other words, your imagination is your friend.

Here are some 'training ugly' ideas to get your creative juices flowing:

- **Moving tee after every swing** – up or down, inside or outside. I rarely put the tee right down the middle for my hitters. Just like in the Bean Bag Study…if they can hit the inside and outside pitch, then they'll hit it down the middle.
- **Varied-Reaction-LIVE-Toss-Timing-Drill (VRLTTD)** – my favorite drill for timing. I use two plates set about five to ten feet apart, and throw from a stationary L-screen. I then progress the hitter through the following depending on challenge level…Easy – hitter shifts

plates after every 5-swing round…Medium – hitter shifts plates after every two swings, for a 6-swing round…Hard – hitter shifts plates after every two pitches, for a 5-swing round.
- **Reverse Strike-zone** – I just started doing this with my hitters. Hitter takes a five-swing round, hitting "strikes". Goes through a coach's evaluation, then does a five-swing round, hitting "balls". How does this benefit? This gives a hitter a better sense of the strike versus hitting zone, plus it fries their brain! Also, if you're pairing this with the VRLTTD drill above, make sure to start on the Easy progression.
- **Random-Pitch-Round** – think of the Cal Poly hitters in the random group from the study we looked at earlier. In a five-swing round, I'll mix 4-seam fastballs with either the circle change-up or a knuckleball…to minimize grip change in the glove. OR, I'll mix the 2-seam fastball and the curveball or cutter. The hitter works on hunting one of the two pitches in one round. Also with this, start on the Easy progression to VRLTTD.
- **Working mechanics** – in a 5-swing round, I'll have the hitter work the effective mechanics and its ineffective counterpart. For instance, if we're working on 'showing the numbers', then on the odd swings (1, 3, and 5), the hitter will 'show numbers'. And on the even swings, the hitter WILL NOT 'show numbers'. When doing this, please explain to your hitters you want them focusing on process, not results. In other words, if they 'show numbers' when they're supposed to, but swing and miss, they get an 'A' for that swing. If they don't 'show numbers' when they're supposed to, but hit a fiery hole through the back of the cage, then they get an 'F' for that swing.
- **Barrel awareness** – wind frog-tape around the sweet spot of the barrel, but with about a half inch gap between the tape. Tell your hitter to practice hitting the outside, middle, OR inside tape on all swings or for certain swings. Great drill for increasing batting average.
- **Barrel control** – hit on an open field and put markers out in the outfield, like you'd see at a golf course driving range. Have the hitter practice hitting the different markers in a particular order. They can stride however they like, to accomplish the swing objective. Another great drill for increasing batting average.
- **Hand-speed control** – have the hitter swing using different hand speeds, but still get positive launch angle. The coach throws the ball at different speeds, and the hitter matches. Great for adjusting to off speed.

You can thank Coach Lee Comeaux for the last three, coming from his golfing background, accuracy is EXTREMELY important. His 13-year-old daughter, who plays softball in Texas, hit over .600 in her league this past year with his teachings.

Giving Feedback to Hitters

Think back to when you were transitioning your kids from the bike with training wheels to a bike without…

Did you throw the training wheels away totally, or leave one on, allowing for the young one to lean on the training wheel side for safety?

Here's a clue…

The best way to get kids riding a bike without training wheels is…

Drum roll please…

…to have them ride the bike WITHOUT training wheels!!

Just kidding, I know you knew that. I was just giving you a metaphor for giving feedback to hitters.

Think of the training wheels as the frequency of feedback you give to your hitter or hitters.

If you're constantly reminding them what they need to fix or are doing great at after each swing, then you're the bike with the training wheels still on.

Don't get me wrong,

I'm not saying zero feedback is the best way.

I want to remind you of the Goldilocks Golden Rule we covered a short while ago.

Highly frequent feedback or none at all are not effective; we want what's just right.

What's the happy medium for giving feedback to hitters?

Using our 5-swing rounds as an example…

I do my best to put my poker face on until the end of five swings. Occasionally I'll say, "okay", "alright", or "next" just to let them know to move to the next swing, but **I try to cloak my elation or disgust because I want them to ride the bike without me being the training wheels.**

Young athletes are FULLY capable of making adjustments on their own

I tell my hitters to listen to the little voices in their head…lol

No really…when there's high frequency feedback being given to them by outside sources (YOU!!), then that little problem-solving voice shuts up.

Here's a great example…

In his book, *Golf Flow*, Professor Gio Valiante, a Sports Performance Psychologist who works with top PGA tour golfers, recalls a class session where he teaches at Rollins College in Winter Park, Florida…

In the middle of a class session that was being video-recorded, he asked a female student to walk up and try her hand at sinking a putt on a 6-foot artificial green he had set up.

The first try was rushed, and she missed horribly beyond the cup.

The second try she took more time to line up and her putt came up a bit short.

The third try she took a little more time, made a few mechanical adjustments, then sank the putt!

Please note that during the test, not a word was said to her.

Dr. Gio Valiante then had everyone in the class watch the video back, and analyze what key adjustments she made after her misses.

The key here is that the female student made the adjustments on her own.

I tell my parents, your son or daughter figured out how to walk on their own. You didn't need to coach them. Gravity did. They figured out what stance is more stable, and which step to not make…on their own.

In-between swing rounds, I ask more questions than I give answers. It's like weekly quizzes in school. **Studies show, the more the brain has to work to remember something new, the stickier the lesson.**

The 3 Question Hitting Outcome Checklist

After a LIVE batting practice 5-swing round, I ask the following three questions:

1. **How many strikes did you swing at?**
2. **How many swings were on-time?** And,
3. **How did you do with [fill in the blank] hitting mechanic?**

And yes, in that order.

If they're not swinging at strikes (assuming they're not doing the reverse strike zone drill), then effective mechanics will break down.

If they're not on-time, then effective mechanics will be rendered ineffective.

The common conclusion players and coaches jump to is that a bad hitting outcome in the game is a result of bad mechanics.

Mechanics SHOULD BE the last thing to tinker with.

An example of a checklist question I'd ask in number three above would be,

Let's say the hitter is working on Finger Pressure in that round, specifically top hand, bottom-three-finger-pressure on all swings...

Then I'd ask them,

"What were the top two swings where you turned Finger Pressure on and off when you were supposed to?"

After they answered, then I'd follow up with,

"What was the worst swing, where you didn't turn Finger Pressure on or off when you were supposed to?"

It's important to note, that **this question MUST be skipped during and after game at-bats. Postgame is fine, but not during the game. Coaches, only focus on questions one and two during games.**

If it's not front of mind, then it will be forgotten.

That's the magic in asking these three questions between swing rounds. Some hitters will be more aware of these points than others, but others will need to dust off this part of the brain.

It's rare that I have a hitter that doesn't improve their plate discipline and timing after three 5-swing rounds of asking these questions. The more rounds taken, the better they get.

A coach's main teaching objective is to mold hitters who are self-correcting machines. Take those training-wheels off and let them fly!

How often should young hitters practice and how many swings per session?

I get asked this question quite a bit...

In my experience, **what I've found over the years is 4 to 5 days per week is the sweet spot for practice frequency.**

I ask my local hitters how many hitting homework days they got in during the week prior to this lesson, and if they respond with 1 to 3 days...

With almost 85% certainty. I know we'll have to review what we worked on the week before. With this practice frequency, some hitters may progress in the lessons; and others will be repeating a past lesson.

Looking at the slow-motion video, it's rare to get a hitter that spends less than 3 days with their hitting homework, and 100% progress forward on the next lesson.

How many swings per session is very important.

You've already read about the *Principle of Specificity* and the *Goldilocks Golden Rule*, so you should already have a clue that a hitter can take too many swings.

And obviously, not taking any swings isn't effective either, evidenced in the frequency of practice time we just talked about.

I've moved away from prescribing swings in quantity, to having my hitters work within an allotted time.

I tell my hitters to give me 5-minutes per day, for 4 to 5 days per week. I tell them to be happy if they get their 5-mins in...have mom or dad set a timer, and once it goes off, then they're done and can move on to video games.

Why only five minutes?

I want to set those less motivated or inspired hitters up for success, coaches you know who those are.

I already know the more motivated and inspired will put more time in and that's fine. But the objective is quality OVER quantity swings. Remember, **make every swing count.**

And their practice at home should somewhat resemble our 'training ugly' principles discussed earlier. Deliberate, deep practice as Daniel Coyle says in his book, *The Talent Code*.

Here's what we covered in this monster CHAPTER:

- **How to train "game-ready" hitters**
- How to find out a player's dominant learning style in 5-mins
- How to apply 'training-ugly' principles to practice
- Coaching feedback and practice time: **how much is too much, and when is it not enough?**

21

SECTION 2, CHAPTER 5

LEARNING: Motivating The Elephant

This ONE Evolutionary Trait That Can Ruin Great Instruction

In this section, we'll be going over some powerful – yet primitive – human psychological insights:

- The Rhesus monkey study: presence or absence of a safe harbor,
- The "weapons" focus, and
- Brain will never outgrow its preoccupation with survival.

The Rhesus monkey study: presence or absence of a safe harbor

In *Brain Rules for Baby*, John Medina brings up a baby monkey behavior study that was done at the University of Wisconsin-Madison in the 1950's by Harry Harlow.

In the study, baby Rhesus monkeys were tested in isolation chambers with metallic surrogate mothers – doll like structures serving as maternal stand-ins (both were made of harsh wire, but one had soft terrycloth covering the wire). And both were holding bottles of food.

What was interesting in the study was the babies clung to the soft terrycloth mothers in an unfamiliar room. However, when the baby monkeys were left with the harsh wire mother in an unfamiliar room, **they ran screaming from object to object looking for their lost mother**.

Medina noted:

> *"It was the presence or absence of a safe harbor. Human babies, complex as they are, are looking for the same thing."*

We humans have a primal need to survive. The brain isn't interested in learning.

Let me give you another example, and then see how this applies to coaching youth athletes…

The "weapons" focus

In the same book, John Medina tells a story of a primal lesson one flight instructor learned while teaching one of his students...

> "A former fighter pilot, teaching at an aeronautics university recalled one of his students had been a star in ground school but was having trouble in the air. During a training flight, she misinterpreted an instrument reading, and he yelled at her, thinking it would force her to concentrate. Instead, she started crying, and although she tried to continue reading the instruments, she couldn't focus. He landed the plane, lesson over."

What happened?

The student's mind was focusing on the threat (or the instructor) and not fixing what the instructor wanted her to.

Here's another example of the weapon's focus...

Oftentimes a police officer has a difficult time getting a victim robbed at gunpoint to identify the suspect afterwards. But what's interesting is the victim can identify the weapon involved in the life-threatening situation to the specific detail.

Why is this?

Because the mind is most concerned with survival – and in the preceding cases – the weapon's focus becomes the yelling instructor or the loaded revolver pointed at them.

Our brain's are in the business of **learning to survive, and not surviving to learn**.

How does this apply to coaching young athletes?

Brain will never outgrow its preoccupation with survival

The baby Rhesus monkey study, and the "weapons focus" are examples of a primal connection to the human brain and it's preoccupation with survival. Science shows us humans can never outgrow this.

So what is a coach to do when they can't yell, curse, and use negative criticism?

Well, they'd actually have to communicate effectively by golly! Otherwise, they **risk getting mediocre performance out of their players**. We've already gone over a number of different solutions in the KNOWLEDGE section one of the book, remember talking about...?

- Having clear consistent rules and rewards, swift punishments, and rules that are explained,
- Keeping things simple by using short cue switch-words,
- Praising-for-effort language,
- The four virtues of great coaching: knowledge, playing detective, communication, and theatrical honesty,
- **Perfecting the fine art of empathy,**
- Staying away from hyper-parenting and coaching,
- Utilizing the John Wooden coaching principles, and
- Having organized practices and instilling self-discipline in your players...

If youth athletes – or kids for that matter – don't feel safe, then their brain shuts down the learning process. **It's a scientific fact that babies born in low socioeconomic environments have a lower IQ**. And this fact stems back to Maslow's Hierarchy of Needs. These kids never make it past the red level: Safety (*See Figure 31*).

The same can be said for kids playing on high-fear teams...they make for very non-skilled athletes.

Remember, this ONE primal trait – **fear for survival – can ruin the best instruction**. We talked about:

- The monkey study: presence or absence of a safe harbor,
- The "weapons" focus, and
- Brain will never outgrow its preoccupation with survival.

22

SECTION 2, CHAPTER 6

LEARNING: Shaping The Path

Smart Tips Keep Athletes from Wasting Practice Time at Home

A parent not working with their kids at home is one of the most frustrating things for youth athlete coaches. Especially when the parents **expect their kids to 'auto-magically' get better** just by going to team practices.

Hopefully – by now – you understand the science behind wrapping myelin (duct tape) around nerve fibers (copper wire) in the brain. Because practicing a skill ONLY three times per week doesn't cut it.

The difficult task, for a coach, is getting – already over-scheduled – parents to engage their children at home on what to reinforce from practice.

Here's what I have for you in this section:

- Revisiting the Rule of ONE Focus,
- Ask for AT LEAST five minutes of movement homework per day, and
- A simple trick to making parents more productive with their kids at home.

Revisiting the Rule of ONE Focus

Remember, when we talked about Leo Babauta (from ZenHabits.net), and what happens when we have too many focuses at once?

- ONE focus = 85% successful in learning a new habit or skill,
- TWO focuses = 30% successful, and
- THREE or more focuses = less than a 10% success rate.

If we're going to send our athletes back to their parents with "athletic homework", then we have to keep it simple. If we determine through "Possibility Thinking" that our focus needs to be playing catch "belt-to-hat", then communicate that to the parents. Tell them this is what our team is focusing on this month.

Also, have some easy options for parents to accomplish this at home with what they already have to work with. In other words, don't require sophisticated equipment – and oftentimes expensive – to accomplish your objective.

I used to throw a tennis or racket-ball against an area of my parents house (stucco and brick) to work on fielding ground-balls, when my parents weren't home from work yet.

My eight-year-old nephew, I mentioned earlier, throws a baseball, tennis, or racket-ball against the cinder block wall that makes up the back of his backyard for thirty minutes to an hour at a time.

Make accomplishing a team's objective simple to execute at home. Keeping your strategic plan to one focus appeals to *The Rider*. Now, to get the *Elephant Motivated* (both athlete and parents), we have to…

Ask for AT LEAST five minutes of movement homework per day

Try and get parents to think of practice as just like school homework. Ask your parents to cut out at least five minutes per day, four to five days per week, to practicing the team's skill objective. And this is home practice…away from your practices. Tell them, they can do more, but five minutes is the bare minimum to getting them into the habit of actually 'doing the work.'

Five minutes a day is nothing…considering how much time kids are allowed to play video games, be on the computer, or on a mobile device! In a moment, I'm going to introduce you to an at-home points reward system that will make your parents more productive with their kids. I learned it from one of my teacher parents and use it with my 4-year-old boy.

Remember when we talked about having the best most detailed plan in the world (The Rider), doesn't matter a hill of beans if the elephant isn't motivated? Five minutes a day to play catch "belt-to-hat" aligns with the ONE Focus Rule.

A simple trick to make parents more productive with their kids at home

I thought this was such a great idea, I just had to share it with you. It's a way for coaches to motivate their players and parents with a simple idea.

I wanted to share an at-home point system any parent can put to use right away. This also corresponds with the *THREE Commandments to Coaching a Moral Athlete*:

- Clear consistent rules and rewards,
- Swift punishment, and
- Rules that are explained.

Already in this section, we've *guided the rider*, and *motivated the elephant*. Here, **we're going to define the path, and sprinkle in a little more motivation**. I'm going to introduce a simple reward system. And by all means, feel free to be creative with it…use this guidance as a template.

The main objective is kids MUST learn how to 'earn' things. They MUST learn how-to put forth the effort.

Here are the rules of the road:

- Points (stickers work well), time, or money are earned for doing something productive.
- Explanation of productive and non-productive tasks (the WHY behind them).
- And, the points, time, or money earned can be spent on desired non-productive tasks.

Here are **sample PRODUCTIVE tasks**:

- Reading a good fiction or non-fiction book above their reading level,
- Reading or listening to auto/biographies on successful people (Audible.com is great for auditory learners)
- Doing chores and helping out around the house,
- Finishing homework by a certain time,
- Eating dinner at the dinner table without mobile devices,
- **An hour of being 'unplugged** (no video games, computer, internet, tv, mobile devices, etc.)
- Starting a school project early (not procrastinating),
- Practicing for at least five-minutes on their one focus for your team, four to five days per week.
- Eating their vegetables first, proteins and fats second, and then starches and sugars last.
- **If they don't like to get up or go to bed early, then getting up or going to bed early**.
- Working out on their own time: going on a walk, jog, hill run, riding their bike, doing Yoga or Pilates.
- Participating in another sport that is balanced (i.e. basketball, soccer, martial arts, gymnastics, or dance).
- Playing outside with friends.
- Giving back to the community (i.e. handing out food at the homeless shelter).

You can measure productivity by assigning time to each task. For instance, an hour of pleasure reading is worth fifteen minutes of non-productive task time.

Do what the free airline mile credit cards do: before they get $100 free to put towards a destination of choice, they have to put $10,000 on the card first!

Here are **some NON-PRODUCTIVE tasks**:

- Video gaming,
- Loitering at the mall,
- Watching television for pleasure,
- Pleasure reading (comic books, hobby study, magazines, etc),
- Surfing the internet on computer or mobile device,
- **Cell phone usage** (texting and talking),
- Taking the car out for anything other than school or work, or
- Going out with friends.

For my 4-year-old, my wife and myself keep it simple. He gets a Star Wars sticker (he loves SW right now), if he:

- Is patient with his 9 month old sister, not knocking her down, hitting her, or stealing toys from her when she's annoying him or getting in his way.
- Obeys his mommy and daddy when it's time for him to take a bath, nap, going to bed, or when his video time is up on his Kindle.
- Cleans up and organizes his toys without us having to tell him.

When he gets 10 stickers, we take him to the toy store and get him a reasonably priced toy. You see, he has to EARN it.

You get the idea – use your own imagination. The rules and rewards need to be clear, punishments swift, and rules reasonably explained.

This is such a great **system for your parents to get their kids to be more productive at home**, and it'll definitely transfer to the field.

Remember, in this section,

We guided the rider, motivated the elephant, and shaped the path to discovering *Smart Tips to Keep Athletes from Wasted Practice Time at Home*. We went over three concepts:

1. Revisiting the Rule of ONE Focus,
2. Ask for AT LEAST five minutes of movement homework per day, and
3. A simple trick to making parents more productive with their kids at home.

Now for the last and final section…this is where we apply sticky coaching principles to your practices….

23

SECTION 3, CHAPTER 1

DEVELOPMENT

"If you don't have time to do it right, when will you have time to do it over?" – John Wooden

What's in the DEVELOPMENT Section

Once again, I asked my tens of thousands of email subscribers what the two most frustrating things about coaching Little League were, and here were the common DEVELOPMENT responses coming from coaches:

- Focusing on elite travel players versus developing beginners (Rec. leagues v. Competitive).
- Learning key fundamentals like playing catch, throwing strikes, and hitting to all fields.
- Quality versus quantity of games.
- **Winning v. Development philosophy**: building character v. sustaining reputation.
- Running up the score, crowding the plate, throwing outside, can't hit so encouraged to bunt or walk, hit the ball on the ground.
- Playing Money-Ball…OPS versus AVG.
- Creating balanced athletes in an imbalanced sport.
- 90% of outs should be to first base.

Have you experienced or wondered about any of these? What does the science say?

These were at the heart-and-soul of the story I told about my eight-year-old nephew's all-star baseball game this past summer at the beginning of the book.

I constantly hear these coaching blasphemies from my parents as they're dying on the battle field every day, fighting to go upstream against the raging waters.

As we dive into the following information, I'll do my best to address these common frustrations with what science and the Top 1% of coaches say about them.

We'll keep close to the rider, elephant, and path metaphor as we look at how-to make scientific coaching sticky…

Also, in the DEVELOPMENT section, we'll be looking at coaching efficiency, or 'what to teach'.

We're going to analyze the *right things* a Little League or 12u softball coach MUST focus on in practices. You can call this the practical part of the book.

We'll be developing strategic fundamental MUST's for the Little League level, such as:

- Learn how-to play catch,
- Discover how-to lift low pitches and hit to the opposite field, and
- We'll reveal how-to throw strikes and locate pitches.

Among other tricks to speed up the learning process and make scientific coaching stick!

Learn how-to play catch

As you probably already know, better teams take advantage of inferior teams who can't play catch. It gives these superior teams a golden opportunity to 'pad' their stats. Coaches of these teams get to watch their players – literally – run over teams.

Remember, as one of my Little League coaching dads said, over ninety-percent of batted balls in Little League *should* be outs at first base. Playing catch is a BIG DEAL in developing a successful team.

In *The Science Of Sticky Coaching*, we want to level the playing field.

Discover how-to lift low pitches and hit to the opposite field

At the Little League level, pitchers live on the outside corner because:

- Their afraid to pitch inside for fear of beaning someone,
- They want to stay away from pull happy hitters,
- **Inexperienced umpires call pitches** one, two, and sometimes three ball's lengths outside giving the pitcher a conveniently wide strike-zone, and
- Coaches and pitchers know hitters at this age don't know how to properly hit an outside pitch to the opposite field with power.

One of the Golden Rules of pitchers that is taught at EVERY level, is to keep the ball down in the strike-zone. WHY? So hitters hit the top of the ball, increasing ground-balls. Yes, most 10u baseball and softball teams are very good at playing catch, but what happens when they meet a better team that does? Offense will dramatically plummet for teams promoting hitters to hit ground-balls.

For these reasons, I'm going to share with you the right way to develop your batters to hit with power to the opposite field. I had two hitters this year, one was nine-years-old and the other was ten, hit their first opposite field gap bombs! This is pretty amazing since I didn't hit my first opposite field dinger until my senior year in High School.

Not to mention, Bryce Harper of the Washington Nationals has credited his meteoric rise to MLB stardom on learning how to hit to the opposite with power at age eight!

We'll reveal how-to throw strikes and locate pitches

And, as a pitcher we're going to walk through locating pitches and throwing strikes. As legendary college baseball Coach Bob Bennett said, this is a MUST for Little League Coaches to teach.

Coach didn't say, learning how to throw curve-balls, sliders, or cutters was important. **Learning how-to throw "breakers" are a VERY unhealthy focus for a younger skill level**. Now learning how to hit them, on the other hand, is different. You'll most definitely see them from other teams who aren't keeping a young developing arm in mind.

It's super critical that Little League pitchers learn how-to locate pitches and change speeds in the strike-zone. You'll see hitters, at this level, crowd the plate to compensate for wide strike-zones, AND for an inability to hit the outside pitch effectively.

Pitchers must get comfortable throwing inside and working the plate, and rest assured, we'll address all these developmental strategies shortly.

24

SECTION 3, CHAPTER 2

DEVELOPMENT: Guiding The Rider

> *"Discipline yourself, and others won't need to."* – John Wooden

The Most Critical Role a Coach Will Ever Fill

In this section, we'll be talking about what St. Louis Cardinals head coach Mike Matheny brought up in his *Letter to Parents PDF* (http://gohpl.com/mmlettertoparents) that you can download and read on your own:

- Players need to be taught how to play with Class (Character),
- To respect others (including. parents, umpires, coaches, and players),
- **Players be accountable for their own actions**,
- Come prepared to play (dressed and ready, water, snacks), and
- Practice self-discipline.

Players need to be taught how to play with Class

We can also refer to 'playing with class' as a person's character shining through. Legendary college basketball coach John Wooden said these three things about Character:

- *"Be more concerned with your character than your reputation, because your character is what you really are, while your reputation is merely what others think you are."*
- *"What you are as a person is far more important than what you are as a basketball player."*
- ***"Winning takes talent, to repeat takes character."***

This from a Coach who won ten NCAA college basketball championships in the span of twelve years! I think he's credible enough to talk on the subject of character.

Coach Mike Matheny uses the term 'play with class' or 'be classy'. The Urban Dictionary says 'Classy' is defined as:

"An adjective 1) meaning very stylish and elegant, 2) not crude or disgusting or dirty or depressing, 3) a deeper, more meaningful word for 'cool'."

Sometimes it's hard to take a word like 'character' or 'play with class' and apply it. So I like to **use of human role models that embody the essence of the word as a measuring stick**.

In baseball, you might look at guys like Derek Jetter, Dustin Pedroia, Adam Jones, Cal Ripkin, Don Mattingly, or even Hank Aaron. In softball, young ladies may look up to Jennie Finch, Joan Joyce, Sierra Romero, or Cat Osterman.

As John Wooden says,

"Young people need models, not critics."

Although humans aren't perfect, **have your kids look for a role model who consistently shows great character and plays with class on and off the field**. Urge them to cover their bedroom walls with their role model in FatHead form as a constant reminder.

Arnold Schwarzenegger covered his bedroom wall with posters of American bodybuilders before coming to the US to compete. Steve Jobs had a big poster of Albert Einstein that inspired him. Warren Buffett had Benjamin Graham to look up to when he started investing in stocks.

To respect others (incl. parents, umpires, coaches, and players)

I can't believe I actually have to say this. But today's standards for the youth respecting their elders – let's be real – has withered away like a strawberry in winter. Coach Mike Matheny says in his Letter:

"Coach is always right, even if he's wrong. ***Our culture has lost this respect for authority*** *mostly because the kids hear the parents constantly complaining about the teachers and coaches of the child."*

Or course, there are bad coaches out there. The heart and soul of this book was developed to help change all that.

I think there are coaches who are malignant tumors no matter which way you slice and dice them. But **I also think a majority of coaches just don't know any better**, and would be willing to change if they're shown the right way to do things with proven scientific evidence to back it up.

Don't expose your kids to a coach's misguided negligence because – as we've already talked about – our brain's ultimate goal is to survive, and NOT to learn. Remember the "weapon's focus" and Rhesus baby monkey experiment we talked about earlier?

The brain will never outgrow its preoccupation with survival from yelling, belittling, and negative criticism. **If the brain is always in survival mode, then it can't be learning.**

That being said…

Teach your kids to respect ALL authority figures. That goes for umpires and opposing team coaches and parents, no matter how hard it may be. **And remember coaches, you have the responsibility of being your team's role model**. Use a lot of the tools in this book's toolbox to communicate effectively with other parents, umpires, and coaches because your kids will do just what you do. The little monkeys and parrots that they are!

Be accountable for own actions

We live in a 'victim's society'. Most often people refuse to accept fault, and are stuck looking out the window for the answers to their problems, issues, and challenges. World Renowned inspirational business coach and speaker Anthony Robbins has made many millions talking about *The Power Within*.

Athletes are no different. Look at the PED scandal. **Ryan Braun got popped for steroid use and has yet to have admitted his guilt publicly. Why?** Probably because of legal ramifications…he's afraid of a big fat fine…maybe a lifetime baseball ban…prison time possibly…having to swallow his pride.

Whatever the case may be, he hasn't come clean and become accountable for his actions. He's still looking out the window for having been caught with his pants down.

Admitting guilt for screwing-up is hard…for everyone. That's why not everyone readily admits it.

This lies at the heart of most deep seated issues in the world of youth sports. Are we trying to get the next "W"? Or are we working to properly develop inexperienced motor skills? Praise-for-intellect OR Praise-for-effort?

When kids are consistently conditioned with vague generalized praise such as, "Good job", "You're so good", or "You're so smart", they don't want to risk losing that reputation, and they'll do what it takes to keep it. If it means lying, shifting the truth, or blaming others, then they'll do it. Lance Armstrong, Barry Bonds, Pete Rose, and Alex Rodriguez come to mind…along with Braun.

I once heard being accountable for your actions explained like this…**either you're looking in the mirror or out the window. The key is to look in the mirror whenever possible**. It's about constantly asking the question, "How can I do better next time?"

This is an important thought process for young athletes to enter into on a minute-by-minute basis. If we're involved in a play, then we carry some of the blame, maybe not all, but some. It's up to the coach to decide, not the players.

For example…

Sure, a botched sixth inning play at shortstop causing the winning run to score may be partly the middle infielder's fault. But a coach can probably point to other times in the game when his team's runners were left on base, a pitcher walked seven hitters, or an outfielder over threw their cutoff leading to runners moving closer to home-plate. **Each player is just one spoke in the bicycle wheel.**

Come prepared to play (dressed and ready, water, snacks)

I didn't get this until seventh grade baseball. We had what was called Kangaroo Court, and was the first time we had to dress out in our baseball gear at school, then go to practice shortly after.

If a player forgot his belt, hat, water, etc., then his name was written down by coach, and a Kangaroo Court would be held at the beginning of Friday's practice. **All lapses in judgment would be announced in front of the whole team**, and small fines were paid (something like a quarter for each). All fines would go towards the end of year pizza party.

And guess what, at this stage in my career, I got all my baseball gear ready MYSELF!! My mom and dad let me have that responsibility, so if I forgot something, I learned real quickly that that was ON ME!

The Kangaroo Court did a couple things:

1. Was embarrassing to each individual player because our dirty laundry was aired-out in front of the whole team, and
2. We had to hit mom and dad up for fine money, and the embarrassment of telling them what for.

This got most of us players on the ball really quick. After a few weeks, we didn't need to hold Kangaroo Court anymore because everyone was complying with the rules and guidelines of coming prepared to play.

At the Little League level a coach can do Kangaroo Court, but know that in the beginning the parents will most likely be to blame. But, **stress to your players that they alone should take responsibility for how prepared they are when they come out to practice.**

And if they don't have water, a snack, or are dressed properly, then it is their fault. Again, teach them to look in the mirror and not out the window.

Remember, we're turning ordinary athletes into extraordinary...the difference is that little "extra".

What a coach needs to be clear about to the parents is they need to get them there at least fifteen minutes before practice starts. Not when, as Coach Bennett used to say, *"When your robes were on fire."*

Practice self-discipline

Self-discipline is getting players to consistently practice healthy productive habits. This can come in the form of pre-practice (getting the field ready), practice, and post-practice routines (picking up equipment, trash, and debris).

It could be them doing their five-minute skill practice at home every day. It can be not yelling or giving an umpire a nasty look.

According to Merriam-Webster's Dictionary, self-discipline is defined as:

> *1) The ability to make yourself do things that should be done, 2) correction or regulation of oneself for the sake of improvement.*

Most of the time, our emotions can inhibit self-discipline. Whether we're being lazy or angry because an umpire made a bad call can bring us out of alignment with our self-disciplined routine.

You've learned a lot in the preceding Chapters that falls under the realm of practicing self-discipline. And also, we've discovered self-improvement patterns a coach can develop in their players.

Remember, we talked about what St. Louis Cardinals head coach Mike Matheny brought up in his *Letter to Parents*:

- Players need to be taught how to play with Class (Character),
- To respect others (including. parents, umpires, coaches, and players),
- **Players be accountable for their own actions**,
- Come prepared to play (dressed and ready, water, snacks), and
- Practice self-discipline.

25

SECTION 3, CHAPTER 3

DEVELOPMENT: Guiding The Rider

"If you're not making mistakes, then you're not doing anything. I'm positive that a doer makes mistakes. Failure is not fatal, but failure to change might be." – John Wooden

THREE Ways to RUIN Youth Athletes *(IMPORTANT Commandments Included HERE)*

This section is why – I think – baseball and softball are the most transferable team sports of all. When we look at how-to equip young adults for real-life pressures, this is the best sport to play. If you want to ruin youth baseball or softball athletes, then:

- DON'T teach players that this is a game of failure.
- DON'T instruct players to focus on what they can control. And,
- DON'T teach a simple thought process for self-evaluation.

DON'T teach players that this is a game of failure

If you want to RUIN a young baseball or softball athlete, don't mention they're going to fail in this game. And don't mention they WILL fail A LOT!! In fact, I've heard parents say the following to their kids (true statements):

- *"Why can't you do this?!"*
- *"You hit this pitcher great last time, what's wrong with you?"*
- *"You're hitting like sh#$!"*

"You" statements with zero solutions offered to fix. Terrible. And sad.

This sport is the only one that you'll fail far more times than you'll succeed. I ask my students, if they consistently get three-to-five out of ten right on school tests, what would their parents do to their personal life?

The point is…

This sport is hard. Hitting consistently with power is difficult. Throwing consistent strikes and locating pitches in Little League is also a challenge. And you can add playing simple catch to that list too.

Yeah, these young athletes are still learning…still developing their motor skills. Sheesh, give them a break.

Our job as coach is to relay to our players that failure is okay. **It's perfectly normal to make mistakes. Remind them that myelin doesn't care about who you are, but what you do.** The best way to build a circuit:

1. Fire it,
2. Attend to mistakes,
3. Then fire it again

…over and over.

This is how 'muscle memory' works.

I know I'm repeating myself here, but if players are constantly told "Good job" or "You're so good" – vague generalized praise – then their struggle will be prolonged indefinitely. And they won't be as effective as they can be when they enter the work world.

The benefit of learning how failure plays a key role in improvement is a HUGE life lesson. This equips young adults to function in the real-world. I can deeply connect and network with any college-on-up level baseball or softball player around the world simply because **we share this simple bond of playing in a high rate of failure sport**.

Here's another tip to mentally RUIN young ball-players…

DON'T instruct players to focus on what they can control

Make sure to tell your players that they can change the mind of the umpire through mental telepathy…mind read what a pitcher is going to throw next…and teach them to instruct the sun to change its position, so it'll blind the other team any time a fly ball is hit.

Seriously though, as a coach there are three things, Coach Mike Matheny shared in his *Letter to Parents*, a coach can demand from their players:

1. Attitude,
2. Concentration, and
3. Effort.

Demanding anything else is a mute point because these are the ONLY things a player can control.

Remember, it's up to you as coaches to remind your players that together they make up a team. Everyone on that team has an individual role to fill and a purpose for doing things. For each player, **the execution of rehearsed skills should rank numero uno on the team's action item list**.

Putting a bunt down…fielding a ground ball cleanly and throwing it accurately…pitchers locating pitches…base-runners watching their third base coach for balls hit behind them…fielders wearing sunglasses and/or shielding the sun with their glove on a fly ball…**hitters not throwing their helmets in frustration** after striking out with the bases loaded.

A pitcher ONLY has control over their emotions (attitude), concentrating on the throwing strikes and locating pitches, and giving it their all. Outside of this, they can't control anything else. Not the weather...not the umpire...not what the hitter does with the pitch...and definitely not the errors their defense might make.

The last thing a coach can do that will RUIN youth baseball or softball players...

DON'T teach a simple thought process for self-evaluation

DON'T have a purpose for doing things on the field. Don't let them think a play or two ahead. Let them steal, shove angry bees into empty Coke bottles in the outfield, and run into the dugout crying with a fat lip (true story). Allow parents to have a full on conversation with their kids while they're playing or in the dugout. No matter what, keep praising them for the 'good job' they're doing.

Okay, duh! None of this is good for development. Bad coach! DO NOT pass go, and DO NOT collect $100.

Really...

In Coach Mike Matheny's *Letter to Parents*, he talks about conditioning a thought process in young athletes. **Teach them that they need to have a purpose behind every move they make on the field and in the dugout**. A coach can do this using non-offending body language and an authentically concerned tone of voice:

"What were you thinking?"

When I think of MLB coaches that do this well, I think of Joe Maddon (Rays), and Tony LaRussa (retired-Cardinals). Coach Bennett was like these guys at Fresno State...calm as a cucumber under pressure.

By asking a player *"What were you thinking?"*, it gets a young mind into the habit of thinking one, two, maybe even three plays ahead. **Having fielders get into the groove of playing make-believe**:

- With runners on second and third, with one out, and the ball hit right at me...what do I do with it?
- Runner on first with nobody out, being the shortstop, who's going to cover second if there's a steal.
- If I'm a center fielder with a runner on second base, if the pitcher tries to pick him off, then I need to back up.

These are defensive situations that a coach can work on in practice, and as we'll learn shortly, **we can shrink the field down to focus quality attention on key mental repetitions**.

As coach, we have to stress a forward thinking plan with all our players, even the ones not starting. Asking *"What were you thinking?"* is after the fact, but it primes players to expect a mental 'quiz' after each play.

This gets them into a deeper practice mindset, which is one of the main ingredients to reinforce the myelin duct tape we talked of earlier. **Let them know the brain is like a muscle: the more they work it, the bigger and stronger it gets.**

Remember, I played the devil's advocate in this section, teaching coaches that if you want to ruin youth baseball or softball athletes, then:

- DON'T teach players that this is a game of failure.
- DON'T instruct players to focus on what they can control. And,
- DON'T teach a simple thought process for self-evaluation.

26

SECTION 3, CHAPTER 4

DEVELOPMENT: Guiding The Rider

How-To Force Your Body to Gain a Competitive Advantage

In this section, we're going to talk about:

- Learning life through playing the game.
- The importance of hustle.

These are my favorite topics when discussing the benefit of baseball and softball.

Learn life through playing the game

As you might have seen *The Science Of Sticky Coaching* mantra is:

"How To Turn Ordinary Athletes Into Extraordinary"

A coach must use baseball or softball as a transference vehicle, or a way to teach young adults life through the sport.

Praising kids for their effort over vague generalized outcomes is a first step. You've already seen the studies.

How young athletes learning the lessons of self-discipline, organization, and how-to be leaders are in themselves powerful…even without skill development. You heard this from legendary Coach Bob Bennett – in his early years – having a baseball coach that didn't know where to find the "box of left-handed curve-balls".

By the way, that's a saying we reserve for those who either aren't listening to our conversation (checking iPhone or looking to see if someone more important than you is walking in the room), or who doesn't understand our sport ?

As a coach, your job is to inspire and motivate them to be forward thinkers and to collaborate as a team. Of course, they may have their individual roles to fill, in addition to executing when the opportunity presents itself. All of this is PRICELESS in ANY workplace.

I can go on and on with different aspects of how baseball or softball can teach many important life lessons. But the best one of all is teaching kids that **failure is a natural process to achieve a specific goal**.

That what John Medina says in his book *Brain Rules for Baby*, to struggle IS NOT an option, but a biological requirement. We must struggle in order to properly develop.

Awhile back, I watched my six-year-old niece learn how to tie her shoes in one hour, whereas it took her older brother one week. It was first demonstrated to her by an older cousin, while she continued to fumble with the laces awkwardly making mistakes, the cousin spent about ten minutes helping to correct her, then left her on her own. After struggling with it for one hour, she was able to do it correctly and repeat the skill. Was she frustrated in that hour…YES! But she just had to learn how in an hour gosh darn it!

This is why I love the sport. It's the **high failure rate that makes this game so sexy**. There's a higher calling than just pitching throwing, catching, and hitting a ball. This game is the best at equipping kids to deal with life's greatest challenges.

The importance of hustle

"There is always some kid who may be seeing me for the first time. I owe him my best." – Joe Dimaggio

There are and were Major Leaguers who were known for their hustle on and off the field. Pete Rose (they called him "Charlie Hustle"), Joe Dimaggio, and Rex Hudler.

Coach Mike Matheny calls this controllable factor 'effort'. Sprinting to a position, to the plate, or to the mound does four things:

1. Cuts down on nervous jitters,
2. **Gets the juices flowing**,
3. Quick boost of confidence, and
4. Sends a high octane ready to fight signal to the body (and to your opponents).

It doesn't have to be an all-out sprint (although this is what I preferred when I played). It could be a brisk walk, or even a solid jog. What hustling isn't is walking, or lazy jogging.

Hustling is also backing up plays when you're the off fielder…a catcher down the first baseline on a play to first…an outfielder backing up a play to first, second, or third base…a pitcher racing to occupy home-plate after a pass ball or wild pitch with a runner on second or third…**a hitter digging for second base on a routine popup** to an outfielder.

Hustle alone can speed the game up on an opposing team, putting up a crooked number before they can take a breath of relief. This sucks when it's being done to you.

At Fresno State, this happened to us whenever we played teams like the University of Hawaii. They were a bunch of scrappers, especially when we played at their place. They lulled you to sleep with their Reggae music, 'Hawaiian time', capricious weather, and beautiful tanned hula girls. Then they struck ferociously like a cornered & coiled Cobra fighting for its life!

As a coach, get your players to hustle always. Of all the sports, baseball and softball can be very boring to watch (this is what my wife tells me). Why not make it more fun and enjoyable for spectators and participants to see players hustling on and off the field?

Even though players may not be hot for the idea, **demanding effort is a way of instilling self-discipline**. Remember, self-discipline is the ability to make yourself do things that should be done. Things that our body wants to be lazy with.

We went over how-to force your body to gain a competitive advantage:

- Learn life through playing the game (this creates purpose).
- And the importance of hustle.

When a coach communicates to their players that there is a higher purpose for playing the game, then all of the sudden these young adults assign more importance to the things they can control.

It's not just throwing, catching, and hitting a ball. There's more to the game than that. There's a game within a game. **A chess match going on between the ears. Emotional momentum is shifting from right to left**. We coaches use failure as a teaching tool, and the impact this type of practice has on college or occupational ambition is priceless.

Also, getting your players to hustle in every facet of the game is HUGE. Praising this effort often is the key to your team's development and later, achieving your team's goals.

27

SECTION 3, CHAPTER 5

DEVELOPMENT: Motivating The Elephant & Shaping The Path

THREE of the Biggest Secrets to Sticky Coaching

I'm going to reveal a few coaching ninja tricks I've learned and applied in my own instruction, from reading Daniel Coyle's book *The Talent Code*, peppered with information from W. Eric Cobb D.C. of Z-Health Performance:

- Shrinking the game down,
- Four paths to movement efficiency, and
- Making a deep connection.

Shrinking the game down

It's an easy concept really. This all started when Daniel Coyle stumbled upon a Brazilian soccer game called Futsal. Please search it on YouTube. Basically, it's soccer shrunken down to a quarter of a regulation field with half the players. So instead of eleven players on one team, only five or six play at one time against another team's five or six.

Coyle was looking for reasons why the Brazilians lead the world in overall World Cup victories, and how come they consistently compete as one of the best in the world year in and year out.

It all comes down to – Coyle says – **firing those circuits faster**, more frequently, and in a very concentrated space to reinforce the nerve fibers with myelin better (muscle memory duct tape).

When you have a very small space to play soccer in with crowded real estate to work with, the brain has to figure things out quickly.

In this midst of firing nerve fibers on the Futsal soccer field, there's massive feedback being generated…when a player gets 'juked' out of his gourd, he's forced to fix the defensive mistake he made or risk constant ridicule.

This is why a guy like Ronaldinho seemed to perform gravity defying soccer ball stunts when he was cornered by three defenders. To spectators, things happen so fast, but to Ronaldinho, things are working in slow motion **because his brain has been trained to process the information at a much faster rate**.

Remember coaches, it's not about the body, it's about wiring the circuitry correctly in the brain. In his research, Daniel Coyle says that the mental reps are far more important than going full speed – or in our case, distance – when we're trying to connect the dots, say on bunt defenses, first and third plays, and relays.

FIVE WAYS to compress and speed up the game:

1. Cut the field in half when doing bunt defenses, relays, first and third plays, and pitchers around the infield. You **don't even have to use a ball – the mental part is all that counts**. Start with a slow tempo and as skill execution gets more efficient, then speed up the pace.
2. For hitters, set up your L-screen at twenty to thirty feet and throw or toss batting practice from there. Three great benefits to this: 1) Easier on the arm, 2) More consistent strikes, and 3) Better throwing control to work corners. **You can also decrease reaction time by throwing harder from a shorter distance**.
3. Have pitchers work short-distance bullpens, either flat ground or on a portable mound, by throwing this shortened distance to hitters (you're killing two birds with one stone here). Whiffle Ball and playing Pepper would be great for this!
4. For base running, providing your goal isn't conditioning but rather mental repetitions, **practice 'cornering' the bases correctly, cut the field in half and have the players walk the correct route**, then progress to a jog, then to a sprint.
5. For groundballs and fly balls infielder and outfielder practice, start by rolling or tossing the ball from close range (split players up into pairs), so players can work on desired footwork. Once they execute the skill at close range, then speed up the tempo at close range.

The possibilities are endless, and feel free to be creative here. These are just some suggestions, and I'd love to hear what's working for your team.

The whole idea of shrinking down the game is to get the players to fire the circuit, tend to mistakes, and then fire it again, over and over. **It's all about 'doing' more frequently here. Use tempo to raise the level of difficulty in tight quarters**. If there are too many mistakes, then slow the tempo down.

Also, let them know, it's okay to slow the movements down until they can execute cleanly. The brain has to catch up with the body.

Do you know what else is good?

Have players watch and experiment high level player movements. Imitation is what players did in the old days when high speed video analysis wasn't available. It's not a coincidence Babe Ruth's swing looks like 'Shoeless' Joe Jackson's.

Which brings me to…

Four paths to movement efficiency

Shrinking down the game is great for developing thick myelin insulation for firing nerve fibers. But what we as coaches sometimes forget is the invisible battle that's going on with athletes and gravity.

You see, gravity is acting on our bodies at all times. I often describe seeing a beautiful swing with my eyes like how the United States Supreme Court Justice Potter Stewart described his threshold test for obscenity in Jacobellis v. Ohio in 1964 as,

"I know it when I see it."

We know a great swing when we see effective movement. We may not understand, but our eyes and brain do. It's part of a primal instinct that was needed when our survival depended on spotting the weakest animal to kill, so our species could eat.

Watching Robinson Cano, Josh Donaldson, and Miggy Cabrera, we see friction-free movement, we just can't explain it.

Dr. W. Eric Cobb of Z-Health Performance describes the four paths to movement efficiency like this:

1. **Perfect Form**– *"The body ALWAYS improves at EXACTLY what we practice."* Good or bad. Focusing on the 'perfect rep' with the above four elements in mind, is the quickest path to a friction-free execution.
2. **Dynamic Postural Alignment**– *"Proper posture increases your spinal stability, provides the perfect torque converter to transfer power from your trunk to your limbs, and decreases your risk of injury. Can you maintain your posture while in motion?"* Look for a Rolfer (Rolf.org), a Chiropractor who can dead-lift more than you, and/or a proven Physical Therapist to better this.
3. **Synchronized Breathing**– In today's scientific movement literature, we're finding that breathing is more and more important to efficient movement. Breathing has to be natural and not forced. When breathing is forced we tense secondary muscles in the upper traps, neck, and jaw. Check out the breathing based meditation apps *Headspace* or *Calm* to better this.
4. **Balanced Tension & Relaxation**– *"Most people are unaware that the one critical element that separates great physical performers from everyone else is their ability to quickly and smoothly move between these two states."* A good strength and conditioning coach like Charles Poliquin or Paul Chek can help better this.

The crazy part is that the "Path to **Inefficiency**" follows these guidelines in reverse order. Tension leads to a breakdown in breathing pattern…then posture starts to falter because the brain is focusing more on protecting the body's joints (spine engine primarily), and the last domino to fall is form. This can all start with an unstable setup.

It's important for a Sticky Coach to understand the four paths to movement efficiency, so when you start to speed up the tempo on a compressed playing field, and you begin to observe your players' execution getting sloppy.

Remember, work on shaping flawless form first, then good posture, then breathing, and lastly the tension/relaxation relationship with the players' muscles.

Making a deep connection

One of my favorite challenges with a new hitting student is making a deep connection as soon as possible. My goal is to make another friend. Ultimately, I become a mentor to them, but I have to get them to drop their guard and get the athlete to trust me. If a young athlete doesn't trust the teacher, then the coaching won't stick.

Back to Daniel Coyle's research in *The Talent Code*…

You can also revisit the KNOWLEDGE and LEARNING sections earlier in this book, but in a nutshell, here's a review on **how-to make a deep connection**:

- Teach in quick informative bursts,
- Target each player and find out how to connect, and
- When done correctly – stop them – and tell them to remember that feeling, visual, or sound.

Teach in quick informative bursts

If you want an athlete to do a certain movement, don't ask their permission first. In other words, don't say something like,

> *"Can you please put your front foot here and your back foot there?"*

Command them with confidence like this,

> *"I want you to put your front foot here and your back foot there. Here's why…There you go, you did it."*

You're the adult – and coach – here. Being able to take ALL the information we've talked about in the preceding Chapters, and melt it down into cues or switch-words can be difficult.

But know this, the more familiar you get with the information, **the better you'll get at digesting large quantities of information**, and melting the main ideas down to the essentials. Remember, myelin works for thought patterns as well.

The main goal of *The Science Of Stick Coaching* book is to present the principles, or psychological/sociological/biological laws of the universe. If you have proven scientific principles, then developing the methods are simple once you know the rules.

AND, also allows you to break the rules at certain strategic times.

Target each player and find out how to connect

Try to figure out what makes them tick…what their hobbies are. Find out what they like to do with their non-productive time (video games, surfing YouTube, etc.). There might be a nugget there to draw a connection with.

The idea is to anchor fun and learning. For example, if a player has fun playing soccer (or any other sport), then I'll tie familiar movements into hitting ones.

I always like to ask how my students' grades are in school. This gives me a good indication of whether they do their homework or not…do they put in the hard work.

I was a terrible test taker. But I was a work horse. I graduated high school with a 4.06 GPA, and a 3.4 GPA in college because of the hard work I put in. It definitely wasn't based on my test scores!

Also, revisit the Chapter where we talked about how to reveal your player's learning style in less than 5-minutes…HINT: it had to do with their eye movements.

When done correctly – stop them – and tell them to remember that feeling, visual, or sound

This is so important. This is the difference between the player just going through the motions, and actively learning a new skill or thought pattern on a deeper level.

Feedback is the name of the game, and it comes in many forms:

- **Physical objects** – a mirror, ball markers on the ground, hitting aids.
- **Video analysis** – video is a great for visual feedback
- **Coach** – this is the best feedback an athlete can get of all.

A *Time* Magazine article dispelled the myth that sitting a baby in front of Baby Einstein videos increases their IQ. The Washington study actually showed the opposite was true – it decreased their vocabulary by six to eight words.

John Medina in his book *Brain Rules for Baby*, said if you want to effectively learn a foreign language, then studying with a real-live person is the way to go. Same goes for feedback with a coach. **Coaches are in a good position to make a positive impression on young athletes. We just have to know what and how to teach them.**

The key for coaches is when you see a youth athlete repeat good form and/or posture, stop them, and make them be self-aware of how different that repetition felt from all the others. This is CRITICAL to deep practice.

I was recently working with one of my high schoolers on quieting up his pre-pitch movement with his hands – up to the stride foot landing. Our lesson was an hour and we probably spent the first forty-five minutes seeking out that one great repetition. And then something beautiful happened…it finally came!

Then it was a mad rush to get him to feel and repeat it again. I was using backward-chaining the whole time, having him take swings on his non-dominant side then back to his dominant side.

By the end, he was able to repeat the correct movement six times in a row. **If an athlete can repeat the same movement more than four times in a row, then you have the beginnings of a change in muscle engrams or patterns.**

According to YourFunctionalHealth.com,

> *"Engrams are like innate computer programs for movement, the neurological blueprints for complex actions. They dictate which muscles will be used, in which order and to what degree."*

So when you get a young athlete to repeat a correct movement pattern, then take a timeout, and get them to store that feeling, visual, or sound into the back of their brain for future reference.

We just went over:

- Shrinking the game down,
- Four paths to movement efficiency, and
- Making a deep connection.

We've gone over a ton of stuff in the book. Now, I want to share a Chapter of my other book *The Catapult Loading System: How To Teach 100-Pound Hitters To Consistently Drive The Ball 300-Feet* (http://gohpl.com/clsbook), on how to address the low pitch…

28

SECTION 3, CHAPTER 6

DEVELOPMENT: Shaping The Path

[Before getting into the Chapter, I want to let you know that one of the most effective ways to get to a low pitch is with the shoulders. The other way is letting the ball travel a bit longer. Timing plays a big part, but if the hitter doesn't use shoulder angles, then it will make consistently crushing low pitches like Mike Trout very challenging]…

> *"Enjoy your sweat because hard work doesn't guarantee success, but without it, you don't have a chance."*
> *– Alex Rodriguez*

Down Gets it Done!

To kick off this CHAPTER, I wanted to share this testimonial with you…

It's from a Florida father, talking about his – at the time – 13yo fast-pitch softball daughter, who I trained in my online video hitting lessons program *The Feedback Lab*:

"Hey Coach,

*It has been way too long but I wanted to share some information that happened yesterday. We are heading up to Chattanooga, Tennessee, the largest showcase in the southeast today. Yesterday was our last day to hit before the showcase and **Mia was struggling with her power**. We hit about 60-70 balls and Mia was hitting about 10% over the fence (she is usually 40%+). I was looking to make sure she was showing her number, which she was, hiding her hands, which she was, landing with a bent knee, which she was and etc., etc. It was getting late and we had to go and I told Mia she had only 6 balls left. I told her to show me her stance and I noticed that her front shoulder was equal to her back shoulder. I then told her to lower her front shoulder and raise her back one. That was the only change we made to her swing, Mia then hit the next 6 balls over the fence and 2 of them were bombs. **I cannot believe the difference this one small change made.***

Thanks,
Primo"

Let me just say, before giving any instruction to Mia, she was doing well. *The Catapult Loading System* just amplified what she already had going for her. And by the way, she's a SUPER hard worker.

I can't stress the following enough…

How well this system works for BOTH baseball and softball hitters.

NOT 7 year-olds versus 24 year-olds…NOT boys versus girls…NOT big versus small bodies…and NOT elite hitters versus amateurs.

We're talking humans here.

A word of caution before we dig into the role of the shoulders in the swing coaches,

Make sure you keep the Goldilocks Golden Rule in mind…

Again, we can do it too much, or like in most cases, not at all.

One of the following Zepp-swing-experiments I did was testing the effect of Downhill Shoulders as close to landing as possible versus keeping the shoulders level as close to landing as possible.

The post analyzed one of the best hitters at using, *The Catapult Loading System*, Downhill Shoulders specifically, **Miguel Cabrera, whose shoulders get to about an 8-degree down-angle pre-landing**.

The title of the post was, *"Baseball Swing Load: If You Can Bend Sideways You Can Gain 4-MPH Bat Speed"*.

Here's a link to this swing-experiment:

http://gohpl.com/downshouldersexperiment

The two big benefits I observed when comparing the Zepp metrics were a:

- **4-mph average increase in Bat Speed at Impact with Downhill Shoulders** versus level shoulders at landing, and
- **3-degree increase in a positive-barrel-Attack-Angle with Downhill Shoulders** versus level shoulders at landing.
- **BONUS: Time To Impact decrease** of an average of .003 seconds with Downhill Shoulders

I take some of my hitters through a visual exercise, where I have them pretend to be standing on top of a small hill, and the pitcher is pitching to them from the bottom, and that's where the coaching cue 'Down Shoulders' was born.

Now, I know you're asking yourself these questions…

Why? What's going on here?

This goes back to Dr. Serge Gracovetsky's *The Spinal Engine*.

Remember the three possible spinal movements referenced by the Physics and Electical-Engineering Professor…?

    1. **Extension/Flexion** (arching, a la Upward Facing Dog Pose OR crunching, a la Hollow Position)
    2. **Lateral Flexion** (aka side bending)
    3. **Axial Rotation** (shoulders moving opposite pelvis)

Here's a clue – Lordosis in the lower-back (#1) is already present, or if the hitter starts in the Hunched Posture, which I recommended in CHAPTER 7, then we've checked Flexion (#1) off our list instead.

'Showing Numbers' allows us to pre-load the torso and take slack out of the system (#3), **but it's Side-Bending (#2, aka Downhill Shoulders) that really initiates explosive Axial Rotation (#3) into impact**.

I mentioned this observation in CHAPTER 5 of this book, but it's worth circling back to illustrate the point…

What we should see in a safe and effective Spinal Engine is:

1. The shoulders start in a downhill angle, as close to landing as possible (between six to ten-degrees *down* gets it done),

2. As the turn starts, the shoulders will flip, for instance, a right-handed hitter's right shoulder will start up, then at the beginning of the turn, it flips down, and THEN

3. During the hitter's follow-through, we will see the shoulder angle flip back to how it started with the right shoulder up, but twisted around.

Think about the beautiful finishes of Ted Williams, Mickey Mantle, and Lou Gehrig.

Now, let me be clear here…

When the hitter begins weighting their front leg, the shoulders will be about *level*, not down.

However, **I coach my hitters to hold the shoulders down to 'as close to landing as possible'.**

The hitters that have the biggest challenge with this, are ones angling the shoulders up when the weight shift releases to the front leg, and most likely are over-rotating their upper torso too soon.

Now, let's discuss coaching out of extremes…

Coaches BEWARE!!

The American way of, if a little is good, then A LOT will be better…DOES NOT apply here.

Hitters will test motor skill extremes, and sometimes they'll stick.

For example,

One of my hitters, 13-year-old, Mikey, who I've worked with since he was 7-years-old…

In his last tournament, on a Little League diamond in Cooperstown,

Out of 12 games, he hit 9 homers, 4 were Grand Slams, and one of the dingers traveled well over 270-feet!

Oh, and he didn't just hit homers, his batting average was something like .700 for the tourney.

It didn't matter if a pitcher with above average or below average stuff came in, he CRUSHED.

He did well this season, with many multi-homer games and near cycles, but never put together an insane offensive output like that.

So, what led up to that week?

That **whole season was a challenge for him timing-wise.**

You see, he's younger for his age, and attends a K-8 school, so he started the year hitting off 60-foot mounds…

Then switched to Pony Rule 50-foot mounds…

Then switched back to Little league 46-foot mounds…

We do train this variance in the cage, but I'm not sure how much he did on his own time.

Long story short,

We did two things…

Number one,

We did a two-plate drill that you'll learn in the last CHAPTER called the **Varied Reaction LIVE-Toss-Timing-Drill that calibrates a hitter's timing**.

I made this drill so challenging for him 3-4 weeks leading up to the Cooperstown tournament.

And number two,

We had to scale down his shoulder angle (pardon the pun).

In other words, he had too much of a Downhill Shoulder angle, **resulting in an extreme uppercut and hole in his swing with pitches up in the zone.**

He was venturing into the 14-degree plus territory!

…Like a golfer, which is fine, because they don't have to hit golf balls above their knees.

So, how did we scale down Mikey's extreme shoulder angle?

The following coaching cue works, whether we're talking an extreme down-shoulder-angle like Mikey's, level shoulders, or sometimes, even up like so many young hitters nowadays.

We use the back elbow as a brain reference point to adjust the shoulder angle.

Wa??!

Why not manipulate the shoulders!?

For some reason in the past, when I've tried coaching the shoulders and not the back elbow, **the message occasionally got lost in translation and the mechanical changes were inconsistent for Downhill Shoulders.**

An example of this was, I would tell my hitter to 'tuck the front shoulder inside the front hip' before landing, and with some hitters it would work, but with most, it wouldn't. Some new hitting flaw would pop up.

I've heard other coaches, like Primo Buffano, in the testimonial at the beginning of this CHAPTER, say, *"lower your front shoulder and raise the back one"*, and *"lower your front armpit and raise the back one."*

My 13yo Hitter Mikey with his "Healthy" Downhill Shoulder Angle

Anyway, I've had minimal challenges with coaching the back elbow.

So, as a general rule, I cue my hitters to get their back elbow up to either level with the top hand or slightly above it, as close to landing as possible.

And this will depend on where the hitter naturally gets their hands to at landing, and just before the turn initiates.

For instance, if the hitter lands with hands held higher, then you don't want to coach them to get the back elbow higher…

WHY?

Because now they'll have an extreme down-shoulder-angle.

So, what I'd do in this instance, is lower the hands in the stance, and get them to move the top hand to not much higher than the back shoulder before landing.

That way, once we move the back elbow up, the down shoulder angle falls within our 6-10 degrees down range.

Again, this Chapter was taken from my other book *The Catapult Loading System: How To Teach 100-Pound Hitters To Consistently Drive The Ball 300-Feet* (http://gohpl.com/clsbook).

Now, let's address how to get players to play catch…

Mikey with Level Shoulders

29

SECTION 3, CHAPTER 7

DEVELOPMENT: Shaping The Path

If You're Not Playing Catch With Deeper Practice, Then You're Losing

The objective of this Chapter IS NOT to go into the specifics of throwing mechanics. It's to offer advice on how to take the learning principles you just absorbed, and transfer them into drills to get your players throwing more effectively.

What we'll talk about here:

- The Sooner You Practice "Belt-to-Hat" the Better, and
- Discover the "Training UGLY" Secret to Throwing.

The Sooner You Practice "Belt-to-Hat" The Better

I first learned this from Coach Mike Batesole at Fresno State, who was the coach when the Bulldogs won the College Baseball World Series in 2008. I played under him for one year in 2003. His first year was my last year.

If I received a penny for each time I heard Coach Batesole remind us about "Belt-to-Hat" after an ineffective throw during practice or games, then I'd be a millionaire.

This was certainly a MAJOR focus for us at the Division-1 college level, so why not at the 12u softball or Little League levels.

What does "Belt-to-Hat" mean?

Just as it sounds...ALL throws MUST be between the receiver's belt – or waist – and hat.

Listen, players' throws will get better when they are forced to throw to a fine target. Just throwing at a target with a broad focus will not win over the long run.

Look at it this way, does a Navy Seal Sniper have a broad or fine focus on his target? His scope narrows in on a specific area of the body for the "kill shot".

Us coaches should promote a finer focus when playing catch. And to up the challenge, have consequences for each throw that doesn't make it "Belt-to-Hat".

Discover the "Training UGLY" Secret to Throwing

If you remember in Section 2 we went over the power of variance, or Training Ugly.

Recent studies in basketball, baseball, and golf show Random Training (also known as Training Ugly, Goofy, or Varied) **has a better motor skill retention and transference rate into games** than Block Training (aka. Massed Practice).

So, how do we utilize the science of successful learning in throwing?

A study mentioned in the Peter C. Brown's book *Make It Stick*, split up a class of grade-school kids into two groups. Group A practiced throwing beanbags into a bucket three feet away. Group B practiced throwing beanbags into two buckets, one 2-feet and another 4-feet away, and with NO 3-foot bucket. At the end, they were all tested throwing beanbags into a 3-foot bucket. Any guess who did better?

Group B. Why?

Their brain had more points of reference to pull from. *"Throw a little farther than two, but less than four."* Whereas Group A had only one option.

Here's what I would do with infielders throwing across the infield to the first baseman…

I would have three separate first bases at three different distances and/or depths, and have the first baseman rotate after each ground-ball or play, giving infielders a "different look".

To make this easy, have the first baseman start and end at the base before hitting the ground-ball, so the other infielders can plan their throws accordingly. To make this more challenging…hit the ground-ball and then have the first baseman actively settle into a base. You'll see how this can get quite difficult in a moment.

Now, let's set up first base at different locations…

You can leave the official first base, but then add another 5-feet up the right field line, and another 5-feet towards home-plate on the first base foul line. Now that would vary the throwing distance.

You can leave the official first base, but then add another 5-feet behind the official one towards the first base dugout, and another 5-feet closer to the infielders. That would vary the throwing depth.

You can even include all six locations and depths. Basically like a random "shoot-around" session on the basketball court.

It's the Bean Bag Toss Study come to life!!!

If and when I coach the baseball and softball teams of my kids, we will be doing this every practice, in addition to the reminder of "Belt-to-Hat".

What we just discussed:

- The Sooner You Practice "Belt-to-Hat" the Better, and
- Discover the "Training UGLY" Secret to Throwing.

Now, let's look at how to use these same learning principles for throwing strikes and locating pitches…

30

SECTION 3, CHAPTER 8

DEVELOPMENT: Shaping The Path

The Lazy Coach's Way To Pitching Success

As I said in the last Chapter, the objective of this Chapter IS NOT to go into the specifics of mechanics. It's to offer advice on how to take the principles you've learned in the preceding pages, and transfer them into drills to **get your pitchers more effective at throwing strikes and locating pitches**.

What we'll talk about here:

- Throwing Curve-balls may be Dangerous to Young Athletes,
- There's Big Results in Effective Velocity, and
- The Quickest & Easiest Way to Pitching Command.

Here's the deal…

I teach my hitters to elevate the ball. To strike the bottom half of an incoming pitch. So, if you want to make it a challenge for my hitters to do this, then keep the ball down in the zone, and get hitters hitting ground-balls. In the Big Leagues, FanGraphs.com metrics show **ground-ball pitchers are much more effective at keeping the other team's run scoring down than fly-ball pitchers**.

And yes, at the lower levels, this will depend on how well your defense can field and play catch. The best teams at EVERY level know how to play catch. Can I get an Amen on that from coaches who've experienced this?! If they don't, then they better be scoring a boat load of runs to make up for it.

And the other thing the best teams at ANY level will have the ability to do is pitchers throwing more strikes and locating their pitches exceptionally well. If you want to compete, then you MUST help your team get better at these things. Just as legendary Coach Bob Bennett suggested at the beginning of this book.

Throwing Curve-balls may be Dangerous to Young Athletes

If you're coaching Little League baseball, then please don't allow your pitchers to throw any kind of breaking ball. I can already tell some of you reading this are shaking your head or rolling your eyes.

Yes, other teams will throw them, so your hitters MUST learn how to hit them. But don't allow your pitchers to throw them.

Please read: *The Arm: Inside the Billion-Dollar Mystery of the Most Valuable Commodity in Sports*, by Jeff Passan.

Throwing curve-balls at such a young age is an ARM HEALTH ISSUE. If you don't agree with this, then ask yourself a question...WHY do you feel throwing curve-balls at 8, 9, 10, 11, and 12 years old is necessary? Is it because you want to compete and win? In Little League, **your best interest as a Sticky Coach lies with your young developing athletes, NOT with your ego or reputation**. Growth Mindset remember? In the grand scheme of things, Little League championship don't mean a thing, unless it's the LL World Series.

How do pitchers like a Greg Maddux compete? This type of pitcher is a pitcher, NOT a thrower. With throwers, it's all about high velocity. Let me ask you this...what adjustments was Roger Clemens FORCED to make when his "plus" fastball wasn't "PLUS" anymore? He became a pitcher. He developed and relied more upon his sinker (to get ground-balls), locating pitches, and changing speeds than he did on trying to blow a fastball by a hitter – like he did in his youth.

Here's my point...

The name of the game here is to upset a hitter's timing...PERIOD.

Putting limitations on pitchers will force them to be more creative with their resources. If you don't allow them to throw breaking stuff early on, then this forces them to LEARN HOW TO PITCH! They'll become more effective locating pitches and changing speeds. **If they're gifted to become a flame thrower, then at least they've learned to be a pitcher early on, therefore making them a double-threat, like Nolan Ryan was.**

Pitches that should be allowed in Little League are:

- 2 and 4-seam fast-ball,
- Any kind of change-up, and the
- Knuckle-ball.

By the way, Clayton Kershaw has gone on record saying if he has a son, that he won't let him throw one curve-ball until he's 16 years old.

Additionally, **speeding up and slowing down a pitcher's delivery and mixing pitches well** can also work to upset a hitter's timing.

Which brings me too...

There's Big Results in Effective Velocity

Perry Husband at HittingIsAGuess.com is an outstanding resource showcasing his *Effective Velocity* system, and I highly recommend you check it out. This is the future of effective pitching. Tell him you heard about him in this book and that Joey Myers sent you.

Here, I just want to make you aware of the Effective Velocity power.

In Perry's research, he's found there are different "perceived velocities" to the hitter. For example, a pitch up and in to a hitter can be perceived 3 to 6-mph FASTER than a pitch right down the middle. Also, a pitch located low and away can be perceived by the hitter to be 3 to 6-mph SLOWER than a pitch right down the middle.

This would represent a right-handed batter from pitcher's perspective, and a left-handed batted from catcher's perspective. Photo courtesy: HittingIsAGuess.com

For example, **if the pitcher registers 90-mph a radar gun right down the middle, that same pitch located up and in may look 93 to 96-mph to the hitter**. And the reverse is true for the low and away pitch.

What does the Effective Velocity system upset? The hitter's timing!!

This is another great way to pitch effectively WITHOUT having to throw one curve-ball.

The Quickest & Easiest Way to Pitching Command

Remember back to the Bean Bag Toss Study again. What do you think a pitcher – and catcher – can do to get command of pitch location using variance or Training Ugly?

Right! Continually moving the gloved target around, and putting a reward point system – or consequence – on the success or failure. **Just to give you a clue, human beings are driven more by punishments than rewards.** To supercharge your points system, you could bring in social pressure like posting the pitchers' points for all to see in the dugout. Or hold a Kangaroo Court for the consistent "losers". This isn't a pass to demean and bully tease here. Keep it fun.

But **there MUST be consequences for those pitchers who don't make adjustments and get better**.

With this reward system, don't you think your pitchers would get better at locating pitches over time? Don't you think if a pitcher keeps ending up in the bottom three that they'd maybe put some of their own practice time in at home? Would this be motivating?

Just like Coach Mike Batesole was a stickler about fielders throwing "Belt-to-Hat" during practice and games, you too must be a stickler with your pitchers. As second to none business development coach Tony Robbins says,

> *"Where focus goes energy flows."*

If coaches aren't serious about it, then neither will the players.

Remember, in Chapter we discussed:

- Throwing Curve-balls may be Dangerous to Young Athletes,

- There's Big Results in Effective Velocity, and
- The Quickest & Easiest Way to Pitching Command.

Now, let's wrap this thing up…

AFTERWORD

I wrote *The Science of Sticky Coaching* book back in 2013 with the intent to turn it into an online video course, and possibly a coaching certification. However, for one reason or another it sat. And to be frank, there wasn't a lot of demonstrable material, and I wasn't confident I could entertain you for over 8 hours discussing this stuff!

I spent months on this project reading, researching, studying, and interviewing. **My fuel was the opening story I shared with you about the grouchy grandfather in the stands** at my nephew's baseball team tournament.

In 2013, my wife and I had our first baby boy Noah, and I didn't give much thought to coaching a team. Fast forward to today, and our young man is now 4 years old, and our family grew once more 9 months ago with a baby daughter.

When I had the bright idea to publish the information in book form, I knew I had to comb through its contents to make sure the info was still relevant to today, while also peppering in some of my personal experiences and my new perspective as a parent.

I probably only changed 5-10 percent of the book's content. To my surprise, all the info was still applicable today, and even more so!

It made me think differently about when my kids start playing on teams however, and hearing the horror stories of my friends, family, and readers coming into contact with these Fixed Mindset coaches. **It's a form of bullying, and I HATE BULLIES. We MUST make coaching American baseball & softball great again!** lol ?

Besides using the information contained in this book, I think another outstanding resource for coaches is the Positive Coaching Alliance (*How to bring PCA to your school or league:* http://gohpl.com/pcatraining). They will help train your coaches, parents, players, and umpires to be on the same page as the principles in this book.

I've aspired to not just coach my kids' teams, but to build a league organization guided by the Positive Coaching Alliance. This is the only way to minimize the frustration of being a coach teaching this stuff, but the people at the top do the opposite. In that case, if you want something done, then you have to do it yourself.

Some of you aren't so lucky, but you can present them with this book, and hope and pray it changes hearts.

Which brings me to what I want you to do for American baseball and softball players...

Spread this book and its message among your fellow coaches. This is a movement, not a philosophy. We're losing thousands, if not hundreds of thousands, of young athletes yearly from baseball and softball because of this BULLY WINNING mentality at the lower levels.

And don't get me wrong,

...It's not about trophy participation either, or where everyone deserves a trophy. Sports are about winners and losers, however **what we're teaching is the process of winning, NOT winning itself**.

Heck, any one coach or player CANNOT with 100% certainty control whether a team wins or loses in baseball or softball. It's impossible, there are just too many variables at play.

Losers should not get anything, except the lesson of what they need to do next time to win. Like the grandparent said, kids must learn to lose, albeit in a praise for effort manner.

All I ask coaches, is that you **keep your mind open and most importantly check your ego at the door**.

If you want to find the Hitting Performance Lab online, then you can at the following places:

- **"Like" us on Facebook** – over 26K+ Likes: http://gohpl.com/facebookhpl *(you can also search "Hitting Performance Lab" on Facebook and we'll come up)*
- **Follow us on Twitter** – 4,500+ Followers: @hitperformlab (or visit: http://gohpl.com/twitterhpl)
- **Subscribe to our YouTube channel** – 4,700+ organic Subscribers: http://gohpl.com/youtubehpl *(you can also search "Hitting Performance Lab" on YouTube and we'll come up)*
- **Connect with Joey on Linkedin** – 700+ connections: http://gohpl.com/linkedinhpl

If you're interested in some of our online video courses *(over 2,000 SOLD)*, then you can learn more at the following link:

http://gohpl.com/hplcourses

If you're interested in the **online lesson training program** *The Feedback Lab*, then you can learn more at the following link:

http://gohpl.com/feedbacklab2

For purchasing this book, I want to make you a deal to get access to all my online video courses with the following…

To purchase FOREVER access to all courses and SAVE $91, then please go to the following link:

http://gohpl.com/webinaronlybundle2

To take advantage of **low monthly access to ALL courses with a 14-Day FREE Trial**, then please go to the following link:

http://gohpl.com/14dayfreetrial2

Make sure that you're swinging smarter by moving better.

And coaches, remember to…

"Go forth and make awesomeness."
– Unknown

HOW TO TEACH 100-POUND HITTERS TO CONSISTENTLY DRIVE THE BALL 300-FEET BOOK

Grab your copy of: *The Catapult Loading System: How To Teach 100-Pound Hitters to Consistently Drive The Ball 300-Feet* book on sale at Amazon today, at the following link:

http://gohpl.com/clsbook

From the back cover:

"My son is 12 and I have used some of the teaching of the Hitting Performance Lab are posting on here and my *son hit the ball over 280 feet several times already in the game, not just practices, and also hit the fence on the fly on 300 feet field, so what this guy is teaching works, a least for my son...He weighs about 110 now but ,what I have noticed is how consistent his power has become thank you so much for your help,* **I played 10 years of professional baseball, and I wish I could of used some of this advice."**

– Sandy Arecena

This book is where Bill Nye the Science Guy meets Babe Ruth. Joey Myers uses human movement principles that are validated by science, to hitting a ball. With this system, **Joey and literally hundreds of coaches across the nation are helping baseball and fast pitch hitters, to consistently triple their body-weight in batted ball distance.**

This Step-by-Step guide shows hitting coaches:

- Why hitting philosophy fails and principles that are validated by science succeed
- Why you shouldn't make video analysis FIRST priority when modeling elite hitters
- What 30+ year coaching experience and pro players won't tell you, and how the information source you focus on can dramatically cut down your learning curve
- **How to become a hitting expert when you've never played higher than Little League**
- There's a BIG advantage to learning how the body actually loads (and it's not what you're thinking)
- A simple method that helped Babe Ruth to consistently crush the ball with some of the heaviest bats ever used
- SPECIFIC elite hitters revealing ways to hit high Ball Exit Speeds, swing after swing, using three elements even a 4yo can understand
- At last, the secret to transitioning grooved batting practice swings into game at-bats is revealed

Go to the following link to grab your copy on Amazon:

http://gohpl.com/clsbook

BOOKS AND REFERENCES

All links go to Amazon...

Positive Coaching Alliance – bring PCA to your school or league (http://gohpl.com/pcatraining)

The 4-Hour Chef: The Simple Path to Cooking Like a Pro, Learning Anything, and Living the Good Life, by Tim Ferriss (http://gohpl.com/4hclearning)

Brain Rules for Baby: How to Raise a Smart and Happy Child from Zero to Five, by John Medina (http://gohpl.com/br4blearning)

The Talent Code: Greatness Isn't Born. It's Grown. Here's How, by Daniel Coyle (http://gohpl.com/tclearning)

Switch: How to Change Things When Change Is Hard, by Chip & Dan Heath (http://gohpl.com/switchlearning)

Move Ahead with Possibility Thinking, by Robert Schuller (http://gohpl.com/moveaheadlearning)

The 7 Habits of Highly Effective People: Powerful Lessons in Personal Change, by Stephen R. Covey (http://gohpl.com/7habitslearning)

Wooden: A Lifetime of Observations and Reflections On and Off the Court, by John Wooden & Steve Jamison (http://gohpl.com/woodenlearning)

The Matheny Manifesto: A Young Manager's Old-School Views on Success in Sports and Life, by Mike Matheny, Jerry B. Jenkins, and Bob Costas (http://gohpl.com/mmbooklearning)

A list of fantastic books on strategy by legendary Coach Bob Bennett (http://gohpl.com/coachbblearning)

One Last Strike: Fifty Years in Baseball, Ten and a Half Games Back, and One Final Championship Season, by Coach Tony LaRussa (http://gohpl.com/coachtonylearning)

The Arm: Inside the Billion-Dollar Mystery of the Most Valuable Commodity in Sports, by Jeff Passan (http://gohpl.com/thearmlearning)

The Sports Gene: Inside the Science of Extraordinary Athletic Performance, by David Epstein (http://gohpl.com/sportsgenelearning)

BOOK CLIFF NOTES

The Science Of Sticky Coaching book is split up into three sections:

- **KNOWLEDGE** (how to teach, doing things right, coaching effectiveness),
- **LEARNING** (how they learn), and
- **DEVELOPMENT** (what to teach, doing the right things, coaching efficiency).

We went over a host of challenges with youth athletes:

- Focus on winning rather than skill execution
- Critical Neuromuscular development time
- Under-prepared coaches
- Scandinavian Study: play one sport = imbalance and burnout
- 1 in 3 children considered over-weight or obese
- Over-Coaching
- Hyper-parenting
- Leaving "beginner" athletes behind
- Is talent born or made?
- Professionals not able to externalize what they've internalized
- Material beats method (falling for the 10,000 hour to mastery rule)
- Raising an immoral athlete
- Nice, easy, and pleasant environment shuts off motivation
- Lack of organization and discipline
- No official youth baseball coaching certification (like youth soccer has)
- Where to START with coaching baseball or softball teams
- How-to build a team culture (creating sense of belonging)

I wanted you to save, print, and pin up the Sticky Coaches Credo:

- **Laying Bricks (& Tracking Results)**: Disciplined steady progress and improvement over time, and understanding development happens at different speeds
- **Wear Your Horse-Blinders:** Motivation to execute a skill rather than win a game, and improve for the 'next level'
- **Come prepared**: *Players*: dressed and ready, water, snacks. *Coaches*: RAMP Warm-up, written practice plan with a purpose (Fail to prepare, plan to fail)
- **Game-play:** Make practice FUN and Engaging
- **'Earn' Your Blackbelt**: welcome the struggle to skill mastery by praising-for-effort
- Realize FAILURE Is A BIG Part Of This Game: Transference = training for life!
- **Operate At A Higher Level**: work on building Character versus Reputation

- **Respect Authority**: coaches, umpires, yours and other parents, teammates, and opposing players
- **Mirrors, NOT Windows**: Look in the mirror rather than out the window…*"How can I improve in this moment?"* Accountability
- **Control ONLY What You Can Control**: Attitude, Effort, and Concentration

Outline to Section 1: KNOWLEDGE

The Art of Effective Coaching ("Switch": Guiding The Rider, Elephant, and Shaping the Path) "Making Leaders"

- o Guiding the Rider
    - **Become Top 5% in Little League Coaches in 6 Months…**
        - *What* study more important than *how* study
        - Principles: Highest frequency material transfer to everything (Ralph Waldo Emerson quote)
        - Effectiveness is doing the right things (how do you know? Talk about Coach Bennett)
    - **How-To Make Coaching Sticky (Three Simple Secrets)**
        - Teaching detailed fundamentals using "trained eyes" (new car scenario or cops and profiling)
        - Take time out for a teaching moment (TC school story)
        - Relentless teaching follow through (Bennett history teacher analogy)
    - **Ask Yourself This Every Practice & Game…**
        - "Possibility Thinking," by Robert Schuller
        - After taking inventory, what's the real issue?
        - Ex. Want to play pepper, but kids can't throw strikes, then take time out for playing catch teaching moment
    - **What Players are Eagerly Looking for in Coaches**
        - Write detailed practices anyone can follow (planning and follow through) – "Fail to plan, plan to fail"
        - Eliminating filler time
        - Skill oriented warm-ups or conditioning (base running, post routes)
    - **Focus on These Two Things If ONLY 4-Weeks To Train for the LLWS…**
        - ONLY 4-weeks to train?
        - ONLY 8-weeks to train?
        - Fine and rough coaching eyes (discuss identity roles of team)
    - **[Story] "That Will Make a Coward Out of You"**
        - Importance of Discipline and Organization over learning skill (Bennett's old coach)
        - Importance of training kids to be self-governing leaders (open sourcing versus central command) – Toastmasters, Al Queda, PD)
        - Kids as independent thinkers & problem solvers (great coaches make themselves progressively unnecessary)
    - **Why Not Use These Coaching Techniques to Your Advantage?**

- John Wooden coaching principles

Best Diplomatic Ways for Policing parents (the up-front agreement)
- Psychology of Hyper-Parenting,
- PDF checklist of parent expectations (or contract?) for coach to print off/send to parents (thank you Mike Matheny)

o Guiding the Elephant
- **The #1 Way to Get Athletes to Listen You**
  - Perfecting the Fine Art of Empathy
  - Describing what emotional changes you think you see, and
  - Make a guess as to wear those emotional changes came from
- **FOUR-virtues of Great Coaching**
  - Knowledge,
  - Playing detective,
  - Communication, and
  - Theatrical honesty
- **FOUR Fool-Proof Ways to Unlock an Athlete's Communication Style (Ability & Temperament)**
  - Low motivation-low skill,
  - low motivation-high skill,
  - high motivation-low skill, and
  - high motivation-high skill
- **The Science of Praising-for-effort**
  - The "Praise-for" study
  - Pros-cons: Praise-for-intellect
  - Five Reasons to Stop Saying "Good Job!"
- **THREE Unique Ways to Ignite Motivation**
  - KISS: don't over-burden working memory, simplicity, over-coaching, Leo Babauta study
  - Address the issue of a nice, easy, pleasant environment and how effort shuts off
  - The Andrew Jones Effect: having someone – a role model – to strive for. To becomes a student of the game.
- **THREE Commandments to Coaching a Moral Athlete**
  - Clear consistent rules and rewards
  - Swift punishment
  - Rules that are explained

- o Shaping the Path
  - **THREE Unique Top Level Coaching Secrets**
    - Using Switch-words…how to teach broad instruction and lead the athlete to fine instruction, simplifying thoughts
    - Backward Chaining: training the 'negative'
    - Chunking (whole-part-whole) teaching

Outline to Section 2: LEARNING

How to Make Coaching Stick

- o Guiding the Rider
    - **The Ancient Secret to Growing a Super-Athlete**
        - What is myelin's purpose
        - "It's not how fast you can do it, but how slow you can do it correctly."
        - The struggle is not an option, it's a biological requirement. Best way to build a circuit: 1) Fire it, 2) Attend to mistakes, 3) Then fire it again…over and over. Working on technique, seeking constant feedback, and focus ruthlessly on shoring up weaknesses.
    - **Movement Studies REVEAL How-To Develop Youth Athletic Motor Skills in FOUR Easy Stages…**
        - Movement Foundation,
        - Guided Discovery,
        - Learning Exploration, and
        - Train with Application
    - **How Transferring Practice to Game Reps Effectively is the Same as Learning a Foreign Language**
        - How to learn a foreign language? Real live social interaction. Pitching machines versus a live arm. Game versus practice swings
        - Data Collection (suggestions, have hitters stand in on pitcher bullpen sessions…have pitchers throw BP)
        - Practice length and frequency
  o Guiding the Elephant
    - **This ONE Evolutionary Trait Can Ruin the Best Instruction**
        - Presence or absence of a safe harbor monkey study. Evolutionary need to survive. Brain isn't interested in learning.
        - "Weapons" focus and study. Learn to survive, not survive to learn.
        - Brain will never outgrow its preoccupation with survival (yelling, belittling, neg criticism).
    - **Smart Tips Keep Athletes From Wasted Practice Time at Home**
        - The one focus rule = 85% successful, two focuses = 30% successful, and three or more focuses = less than 10% successful
        - Appeal to the Elephant: be happy with 5 mins of quality movement practice per day, treat practice like school homework…
        - Define the path: Parents enforcing point reward system at home, keeping an athlete's journal
    - **How-To Make Practices Fun**
        - Benefits of injecting "game play" into your practices: adds encouragement, creativity, energy, culture, and it enables the body to express itself in natural and systemic ways. Studies overwhelmingly show "play" makes everything better.
        - Skill specific games: Last man standing, Belt-to-hat-catch, pepper, Total Bases

- Movement development games

Outline for Section 3: DEVELOPMENT

Efficiency: Doing the Right Things

- o Guiding the Rider
  - **The Most Critical Role You'll Ever Fill**
    - Players need to be taught how to play with Class (Character), to
    - Respect others (incl. parents, umpires, coaches, and players),
    - Be accountable for own actions,
    - Come prepared to play (dressed and ready, water snacks), and
    - Practice discipline
  - **THREE Ways to RUIN Youth Athletes (IMPORTANT Commandments Included HERE)**
    - This is a game of failure. You're going to fail A LOT!
    - Focus on what they can control: demanding their attitude, concentration, and effort
    - Teaching the thought process, "What were you thinking?" Having a purpose for doing things on the field
  - **How-To Force Your Body to Gain a Competitive Advantage**
    - Baseball as a transference vehicle. Learn life through playing the game.
    - The importance of hustle (Joe DiMaggio quote, Ghandi quote)

o Guiding the Elephant and Shaping the Path
  - **Here are THREE of the Biggest Secrets to Sticky Coaching**
    - Shrinking the game down, compress and speed up the game, ex. Futsal, don't even use ball, bunt defenses, defense relays and situations, bp from 30 feet, it's the mental game that counts
    - Slow swing down, have players imitate high level swings over and over, Tempo, Explain four paths to movement efficiency
    - Teach in quick informative bursts, target each player and find out how to connect (re-live FOUR Fool-Proof Ways to Unlock an Athlete's Communication Style (Ability & Temperament), and when done correctly – stop them – and ask them how that felt (teaching moment)
  - **Down Gets it Done!** – benefits of down shoulders when hitting
    - Why? What's Going on Here? – talks about spinal engine mechanics
    - Coaches Beware – be careful with extreme down shoulders
    - So, how did we scale Mikey's extreme shoulder angle? – how to fix.
  - **If You're Not Playing Catch With Deeper Practice, Then You're Losing**
    - The sooner you practice "Belt-to-hat" the better
    - Discover the "Training Ugly" secret to throwing
  - **The Lazy Coach's Way To Pitching Success**
    - Throwing Curve-balls may be Dangerous to Young Athletes

- There's Big Results in Effective Velocity
- The Quickest & Easiest Way to Pitching Command
* Afterward

ABOUT THE AUTHOR

My Name is Joey Myers, and I'm the founder of the Hitting Performance Lab. I played four years of Division-1 baseball at Fresno State from 2000-2003.

I'm a member of the **American Baseball Coaches Association** (ABCA), the **International Youth and Conditioning Association** (IYCA), and the **Society for American Baseball Research**(SABR). I'm also partnered with the **Positive Coaching Alliance** (PCA).

I'm a certified Youth Fitness Specialist (YFS) through the International Youth Conditioning Association (IYCA), Corrective Exercise Specialist (CES) through the National Academy of Sports Medicine (NASM), and Vinyasa yoga instructor…AND, I'm also certified in the Functional Muscle Screen (FMS).

I've spent 11+ years in the corrective fitness field, and have a passionate curiosity to help other players – just like yours – dramatically improve performance through the science of human movement.

I'm currently living in Fresno, CA with my wife Tiffany Myers and two kids, Noah (4yo boy) and Gracen (9mo old girl).

Made in the USA
San Bernardino, CA
19 November 2017